For Patti —
Whom I was privileged
to know as a colleague
and whose friendship
I continue to enjoy.
LeNet and I wish
for you and Jim all
good things in life.
Bay   12/90

Best Wishes,
Julius Parker

GRAB LIFE

AND HANG ON

GRAB LIFE

AND HANG ON

Insights Into the Art of Everyday Living

JULIUS PARKER

HARVEST HILL PRESS

Chattanooga, Tennessee

GRAB LIFE AND HANG ON
Harvest Hill Press / December 1990

FOR INFORMATION ADDRESS HARVEST HILL
PRESS, 340 CREST TERRACE DRIVE, CHATTA-
NOOGA, TN 37404.

ISBN 0-9627915-0-4

PRINTED IN THE UNITED STATES OF AMERICA

FIRST EDITION

To Eleanor
A Precious Gift

CONTENTS

FOREWORD

I'VE LONG APPRECIATED THE FACT that readers of my column thought I sometimes have something to say.

At the risk of sounding immodest, I think they may be right.

I don't say this because I believe I'm any smarter than my readers, or even as smart. My willingness to sound off about life in general is spurred on by being an avid people-watcher.

I watch people with the same interest that investors eyeball the stock market. I pay attention to the "highs" and "lows" of human beings. I've observed them when they are "bullish" or "bearish" or leveling off or drifting or "crashing."

Having had the privilege of "hanging on" for many years and the additional impetus of needing fodder for a column each week, I may have taken closer notice of the human condition than others.

People have been and always will be a source of surprise to me. I've learned it is chancy to generalize about them. Unlike in the old Westerns, there are no clear-cut good and bad guys.

Even the worst of us usually have some redeeming features. This applies to politicians, parents, married couples and those who like hard rock.

Readers over the years have asked me when I was going to put some of my columns in a book. With the nudging and encouraging of my sons, Barry and Steve, my daughter, Eleanor, and my wife, Betty, I finally consented.

I left the choice of columns and editing to Barry. His was the harder job. And he can be more objective.

Hopefully, the readers of this book will agree with the choices. At least my immediate family will have me on record in regard to my likes and dislikes, my battered but still wearable code of ethics and my innermost feelings about life.

I also want to leave them with a sense of my parents' social ethics and work ethics, their Old World roots and values and their appreciation of their adopted country.

IT IS INTERESTING TO ME to notice the change and moderation in my thinking that has taken place over the years in connection with many things, including parenting, women, big shots, the little man, the middle man and people in general. I am still not entirely clear about women, although I count myself as being one of the luckiest of married men.

If I have learned anything in living this long, it is that tolerance and a sense of humor are invaluable assets to taking the bumps out of life.

Also, I have learned that if one lives long enough, one will have his or her share of good and bad times. Life is precious and dear enough to grab and hang on even when the going is the roughest.

Life is for living.

Julius Parker
October, 1990

ACKNOWLEDGEMENTS

THIS BOOK HAS BEEN WRITTEN over several decades and consists of columns that deal with a variety of subjects.

I am indebted to my family for persuading me to incorporate some of them into the book and for getting me moving in that direction.

I thank my son, Barry, a writer and author, for handling most of the editing and publishing details. He was part of a cheering section that included my wife, Betty; my daughter, Eleanor; and my son, Steve.

I especially thank my wife for her encouragement and patience. She is my invaluable lifelong partner and helpmate and the inspiration for most of the good and positive things in my life. I thank her for reminding me to "think book" and to go on with our lives despite painful setbacks.

I owe thanks to our daughter-in-law, LeNet, for gracefully accepting the fact that Barry's devotion to the book interfered with his already busy work schedule and the daily routine of family life. I also wish to thank her for her portion of the typing.

A special thanks goes to the late Roy McDonald, publisher of The Chattanooga News Free Press, and to Lee Anderson, editor and publisher of the newspaper, for approving the use of my column, "Parker . . . and People," in the book.

Thanks goes to Steve Epley, a former reporter of our newspaper who is well on his way toward acquiring a doctorate in English literature. His finely honed sense of modern English was utilized in helping proof this book. Any errors may be reported directly to Columbia University, where he also teaches.

Thanks also to John Wilson, a fine reporter for our newspaper and a published author, with four books to his credit. John's experience with the intricacies of book publishing helped us avoid some of the many snags and potholes that thwart the efforts of producing a book.

A very special thanks goes to our daughter, Eleanor, for her keen personal interest in her dad's book.

How often she lovingly chided her father to "please quit putting it off."

I keenly regret the book wasn't published earlier.

ARE YOU SLEEPWALKING THROUGH LIFE?

I AM CONSTANTLY REMINDED we arrive in this world without guarantees.

No one knows for certain how healthy, wealthy and wise he will be and how long he has to find out.

That's why I'm amazed at how most people seem to take life for granted, especially in regard to good health.

"How're you doing?"

"Okay, I suppose."

"Anything wrong?"

"It's just this darn job of mine. I work for some jerks who don't know which side is up and I get tired of the flak I get."

"Is there something you can do to change the situation or work around those who are giving you problems?"

"Not really. I've got to work closely with them every day. It's part of my job. I've tried different approaches but it doesn't seem to get any better."

Has he thought about changing jobs? "Many times," he said. "But actually I like what I'm doing if it weren't for a couple of people I have to deal with."

In that case, maybe if he'd step back and check out the situation, he would find a change of attitude might do wonders.

IF YOU ARE IN GOOD HEALTH, go to work tomorrow counting yourself among the lucky ones in this world. Most of the time it's easier to change conditions on a job, or at least one's attitude about the job, than to get back your good health.

It shouldn't take a setback in one's health to remind us that good health is not a certainty of life. Nor should anything good in life, including luck, be taken for granted.

A friend says if he wakes up in the morning "not feeling too much pain or anxiety," he gives "thanks" and prepares to go to work.

"Being able to dress myself, drive to work and put in a full, productive day may seem commonplace to others, and for years it did to me.

"But it took on a different meaning and importance when I was laid up in the hospital and couldn't do these 'ordinary' things."

Now they don't seem so ordinary, he said. "Just driving to work is a pleasure. It sure gives you a different perspective."

AWARENESS OF BEING ALIVE is one of the highest forms of intelligence and perception we can be endowed with.

The person who goes through life like a sleepwalker is denying himself or herself the pleasure of savoring what life and its little triumphs are all about. Sometimes the setbacks can even serve to make us more aware of the things that do work out.

But you don't, God forbid, have to have tragic reminders in your own life to understand the blessings of having normal, healthy children and a wife or husband who loves you and is concerned about your happiness.

All it takes is to look around you, to read the newspapers and magazines or watch television and see what you take for granted.

You might also be inspired by the undaunted bravery of those who are struggling to stay alive and enjoy what they can in a world where they have two strikes against them before they come up to the plate.

Some are suffering and bearing unthinkable burdens, but are still willing to hang on for those rare moments of joy or relief from pain.

A FRIEND SAID he has refined the advice to "take life one day at a time." He said, "It has finally occurred to me that every minute we have is a gift. I find being aware of life on a minute-to-minute basis makes it much more exciting and rewarding.

"We not only shouldn't take each day for granted, but each hour, minute and second. Then we won't ask, 'Where did it all go?'"

In effect he is saying there are no guarantees and those who truly know this are the ones who live life to the fullest.

He is also an ardent advocate of the theory: You can't enjoy today if you let it be ruined by yesterday or tomorrow.

There is nothing all that new about this, about perspectives and awareness. Just a reminder you're probably much better off than you realize.

A 'List' Can Be
A Man's Best Friend

WHY SHOULD YOU KEEP a list? Because it's a grownup's substitute for a security blanket.

Not only does a "list" help you keep track of things you are supposed to do, but it allows you to convince yourself you've made a start.

A list is a way of putting things off without making you feel like a chronic procrastinator. It's a cushion to protect your image as well as your flank.

"When are you going to change those filters?" your wife asks.

"I will," you reply. "I just haven't gotten around to it."

"But that's what you said last month," recalls a wife who never forgets anything you've ever promised to do during your entire lifetime.

This forces you to think quickly on your feet.

"I know I promised, but at the time I didn't have it on my list."

But women can be persistent. "What difference does it make if you have it on your list if you don't do anything about it?"

It's at such critical times the list can literally protect you from bodily and emotional harm. That's when you try to make her understand the following logic:

"But by putting 'change air filters' on my list I've actually done something about it. I HAVE made a start."

What in effect you're saying is: If you can't understand that putting it on the list is a step toward getting it done, then that's your problem, not mine.

Nice rationalizing. The next weekend she asks the same question and this time with less patience. After all, she originally made this and other requests a long time ago.

"Please, will you do something about those filters today?"

And here is another one of the crossroads in your life. You either go down to the basement and get the job over with or you stall for more time. It depends on how dangerously you like to live.

For those who live on the edge, the list can once again come to your aid. You tell your wife:

"Tell you what I'll do. I'll move 'change air filters' to the top of the list."

And if you're at least half smart, you'll move back a few steps.

AT TIMES MY WIFE believes I'm a split personality.

Her complaint: "At work you never put anything off, but at home I can hardly get you to do anything."

Why is that? Because at work I don't have the luxury of putting things off. Daily newspapers don't operate that way. There are deadlines to be met.

So when I get home I like to get away from deadlines and from things that have to be done right now.

Doesn't that make sense?

Yes and no. My wife points out she also has to get things done right away at her office and then there are things to do at home which she can't put off.

"I could I suppose not bother to put clothes in the washing machine and the dryer, but then you wouldn't have clean shirts and underwear and socks and stuff.

"I could just put it on a list."

Have you noticed how practical and pragmatic wives can be? And how in making what seems like an innocent statement of fact there lingers the suspicion of an implied threat?

Just as I wrote the above, my wife called to remind me I had promised to help her buy something at the furniture store. I told her I remembered and would meet her.

When I got home that evening, she reminded me "we ought to bring the garden hose inside now that the weather has changed."

I started to say I had "bring hose inside" on my list, but common sense prevailed.

Now let me make this perfectly clear. It may sound as if many demands are being made on me. This is not true. I've just allowed my list to grow too long and that causes a traffic jam of chores. My wife is more than patient with my tendency to put things off at home. I very much appreciate her indulgence.

I hope she accepts my "list" explanation in the spirit in which it is intended. I realize that without her occasional gentle reminder, my list and our lives would become unmanageable.

However, I am serious about such a list. I do have one. It helps.

Now, if I just don't lose it.

THE ONES WHO NEVER 'BEAT THE HEAT'

"How do you keep from worrying?"

I was flattered by the overstatement of the question. If I truly knew how to minimize worry, I'd be rolling in royalties from my record-breaking best seller on the subject of "How Not To Worry."

"What makes you think I don't worry?" I asked.

"Well," he replied, "every time I see you, you seem to be upbeat, in a good mood. I don't see how you can always be that way if you do a lot of worrying."

For one thing, I told him, it isn't good to bring your worries to work. We all have something that bugs us and our worries are seldom unique. Why spill all this gloom into our working place?

That's no way to start or end the day.

Secondly, unless one is almost oblivious to what is happening to him and to others around him, there is no way to prevent a certain amount of worry.

The trick is to keep it to a minimum and not to overdo it. If you are lucky, your Maker will give you a quick mind, one that allows you to punch in to your mental computer, call up your worry . . . and then try to do something about it. If you can't resolve the worry, then quit calling it up.

Of course it isn't as easy to do as it sounds. But if you keep practicing, you'll get better at it. It actually works.

Something else that will minimize your worries is to dwell more on the problems of others.

This will not only afford you a chance to be of some help, if no more than as a listener, but it will remind you that compared to the woes and tribulations of others, you are living a charmed existence.

You wouldn't want to swap and you know it.

HERE ARE OTHER DEVICES I use to cope with worry:

Let's say too many pressures are pushing at you and you don't have time to take care of one before another pops up. At such times I have thought back to a reference point of a World War II battlefield. There were times when I wondered if I would ever get back home alive or in one piece. Our lives were threatened daily and sometimes on an hourly basis.

"Is this also a life-threatening situation?" I ask in regard to the present day "emergencies" which gang up on me at the office or elsewhere.

The answer is: "Of course not, unless I let it become one," and I'm not about to do that.

Another way to stave off pressure at work is to heed this advice:

Do your job as if it is the most important work in the world while realizing that in the general scheme of things, it is only a pimple on the face of time.

This may seem contradictory, but it isn't. It calls for retaining your perspective. As important as your work is, even if you fall flat on your face, it is NOT the end of the world.

Another hint for an ulcer-free yet long and active existence:

Drive hard on the uphill grade but change to a lesser gear when road conditions permit. Learn to relax during such intervals. It will give you more energy for hard work, more staying power and will prevent burnout.

No Guarantees
On Rose Gardens

THERE IS NO SUCH THING as an entirely happy life and the quicker we face this reality the happier we'll be.

I recall my reaction when a philosophy professor made the point that most of life consists of strife and unhappiness.

He must have had an unusually unhappy life, I thought. Why else would he be so cynical and bitter? He didn't say "much" or "part," he said "most."

In retrospect, what makes this reaction more interesting to me is that I was already a young adult at the time trying to make up for some of the five years I had spent in the army here and overseas.

The GI Bill encouraged me and millions of ex-GIs to further our education and to be able to hear words of wisdom from the aforementioned professor and others. I was in my thirties and he must have been about 15 or 20 years older and had also served a tour of duty during World War II.

Did he have that much of a rougher time overseas? No, not so rough. He quite candidly told me in private conversations that his assignment as a major in the Adjutant General's office kept him far behind enemy lines.

So what was it that colored his outlook on life and brought

9

forth his bleak observation that life contained more tragedy than happiness?

For one thing the prof was an avid reader and the numerous books on philosophy and those of an autobiographical nature didn't fail to impress him with a central theme: "Life is a hassle, but it's all we've got."

It didn't escape the notice of this erudite individual that literature, a reflection of life, regardless of the period and age in which it was written, recorded more of life's unhappiness than its happy times.

Also, the professor had lived longer than his pupil and had witnessed more problems and unhappiness in his own life.

"If you live long enough," he said, "you'll fall heir to almost every problem known to civilized man. Most of life is a Greek tragedy."

And when I hopefully suggested that perhaps the happy and unhappy balanced out on a fifty-fifty basis, he smiled tolerantly and said: "I wish I could guarantee that, but I can't."

The French apparently agree with my former professor. They say, "There is no such thing as a happy life, for in order for a life to be happy it has to be devoid of all unhappiness. So, the only thing we have are happy moments, hours and days. Make the most of them."

WHAT THE PROFESSOR also tried to get across was "expect to be hassled, disappointed, saddened and unfairly treated but don't let this make you become sour and cynical."

In other words, if you expect perfection in an imperfect world, you'll be disappointed much more often than the one who sees the world the way it is and is grateful for its respites and occasional happy moments and rewards.

He contended one can be a realist about life and people and still get a lot of excitement and satisfaction from life. Translated: If you lose one race it doesn't mean you can't enter and run in the next. Which brings up a word that is overly used and very seldom acted on in good faith. The word is "fair."

I wish I had a hundred dollars for every time I've heard someone say: "But that isn't fair."

One of my all-time favorite persons has made this statement on numerous occasions.

"Why don't you forget that word?" I suggested. "Just strike it from your vocabulary. There is no such thing as fair or fairness."

The word is too lofty and idealistic to be attainable in its basic meaning. When was the last time you felt you had been treated with 100 percent fairness in any situation? If you can remember such a time, you are indeed unusual and lucky.

But in this tough old world one learns to come up with antidotes and other means of dealing with unfairness and a host of other negatives which plague human beings.

Before you blow your top at the lack of consideration and understanding being directed toward you, stop and think about this old but reliable bit of advice:

Consider the source. Where is that individual coming from? And if possible, don't lose your cool in the first place. Save your energy to think with and to make your next move with.

Whatever you do, think before you react. And never, but never write anything down and deliver or mail it before you've regained your composure after being angry or otherwise overly emotional. "I didn't say that" is much easier to defend against than "I didn't write that."

THOSE WHO TEND TO BE perfectionists have got to have more frustrations and disappointments than their more laid-back colleagues. Perfectionists find it hard to take the advice of those who tell them not to expect everything to go right.

Whether in their personal lives or at the office, these Type-A personalities are bound to take more of a beating because their expectations and motivations are higher than others. They don't need to be pushed or goaded.

These drivers actually wouldn't be happier if they drove slower or were less demanding of themselves. This is not in their nature and personality. Yet they are bound to have more fender-benders and bruises than others because they put in more mileage.

What makes it especially tough for a perfectionist is to be in a middle management position where he or she is literally between a rock and a hard place.

When anything goes wrong, the complaint invariably sifts down to the office of the middle manager. Conversely, when the top man makes a mistake, he can shrug it off with an "I guessed wrong on that" and that is that. Period. End of conversation.

One such middle manager said: "Before I cash in, I'd like to be in a position of having the final word. It has got to take a lot of frustration out of work."

ONE ALSO LEARNS as time goes by to "be yourself" and divest yourself of phony trappings and put-ons. This is one of the few real rewards of hanging around on this old sphere and picking up a little more experience and knowledge.

You learn to finally pick for friends those with whom you can be the most comfortable. The days of name-dropping and trying to create illusive impressions have long gone by the board.

Even the places you go to are selected on the basis of comfort and a feeling of being welcome and belonging rather than of being the "right" place to make a good impression or for whatever the purpose.

Now, you have finally learned, it is time to please yourself and your mate. Everything else is tinsel and show and relatively unimportant.

Be with those you are comfortable with and go where you have a sense of belonging. What a relief not to have to put on the dog for anyone, whether in business or social life. You have learned that is one of life's dividends, and you are gratefully clipping the coupons the years have allotted you.

Instead of squirming and feeling uncomfortable, you are finally beginning to feel relaxed. You have found yourself — the person you have been looking for all of these years.

OTHER THINGS LEARNED along the way:

* Keep a flame of interest and ambition burning, regardless of your age. Have something to look forward to each day and someone to love.

* Be tolerant of your family and friends and others and use a goodly amount of your sense of humor to help you smooth out the bumps and overlook the warts. No one is perfect, not even you.

IT COULD HAVE BEEN
MUCH WORSE

WHENEVER THE HOLIDAY SEASON approaches, I am reminded of when I, as a young reporter, wanted to get a different kind of Thanksgiving feature.

Who would have less to be thankful for on Thanksgiving, I thought, than those poor souls incarcerated in jail and those hapless people who were prisoners of a sort in hospital beds?

I sought out the sheriff at the county jail and asked him if I could have a brief interview with one of the more pleasant inmates, someone who was not doing hard time, but had just erred along the way.

"I've got just the man for you," said the gravel-voiced sheriff. "He's a good man but every once in a while he gets drunk, gets in trouble and has to serve some time."

Brought from the cell was a jolly looking fellow who beamed at me and the burly sheriff. Time for my question: "You don't have anything to be thankful for this Thanksgiving, do you, since you are in jail and won't be out for about 30 more days?"

The happy prisoner kept smiling, and I thought he didn't understand the full meaning of the question. "Can you be thankful for anything when you are spending Thanksgiving in jail away from your wife and family?" I rephrased.

The smiling inmate looked admiringly at the sheriff and stated:

"You bet I'm thankful. I'm thankful that I'm in the finest jail in the United States, with the finest sheriff who ever ran a jail, and I'm thankful I'm eating the finest food ever fixed for anyone to eat free of charge."

The sheriff in turn beamed back at the one who was making these "fine" statements. At one point I thought they would embrace with the emotion of it all. In fact, the photographer got a great picture of the sheriff with an arm around the inmate in a friendly way. Not a choke hold.

"That's fine," I told my interviewee. The sheriff agreed.

As I left I had the distinct feeling this fine, resourceful character would receive some "mighty fine" treatment for the duration of his term.

MY NEXT STOP WAS ERLANGER Hospital where I contacted the administrator.

I explained I wanted to interview someone who was obviously injured but who would recover. It would be a brief interview and not tiring.

I also told him I needed someone whose picture would illustrate his plight on Thanksgiving day.

"I've got the very one," said the cooperative administrator. "He's a young man who was in a bad automobile accident. He's got a bunch of broken bones and ribs and he's bruised all over, but he'll come out of it all right in a few months."

When the administrator took me in to see the accident victim, I could hardly believe my eyes. He was just one huge cast within a cast. His legs and his arms were in casts, as was his neck. He was literally hanging there, with only a small portion of his body touching the bed.

Even a reporter eager for a good feature story was a little hesitant.

"It's all right," said the administrator. "He won't mind. He's a good sport."

I leaned over toward the accident victim: "I'm almost ashamed to ask you this, but do you have anything to be thankful for on Thanksgiving?"

He managed what appeared to be a smile through his facial bandages:

"Sure," he whispered, "I'm thankful IT WASN'T WORSE."

WHEN THE BOY
BECAME A REAL MAN

WHEN I WAS GROWING UP, a boy emulating a man tried to keep his feelings to himself. That was supposed to be the manly thing to do.

I don't mean all feelings were supressed. There was the elation of getting on base, or walking barefooted, or going to a movie or the last day of school . . . and hundreds of other times when you wanted to shout for joy and often did.

That was fine. It was all right to register happiness or sheer ecstasy like during those first dates and the all-important discovery of the potency of a kiss.

You also learned that a show of unhappiness or even anger might come in handy if someone was pushing you too hard and you wanted him to stop.

Many a schoolyard near-encounter had been averted because you unflinchingly stood your ground and steadily eyeballed your opponent and hinted at the dire things that would happen to him if he didn't leave you alone.

It was okay to show these kinds of feelings. After all, a man has got to be a man. A real man doesn't let anyone push him around.

But the problem of a youngster acting like a man became

much tougher when his feelings of pride and person had suffered injury.

Suppose you had just been given six wicked whacks by your principal. All of the above feelings had surfaced, and you wanted to cry so badly it hurt almost as much as the paddling. But a man doesn't cry, although your red eyes tattled on you.

THERE WERE HUNDREDS of other instances when you fought back tears and sobs because you wanted to prove you were a big man on the playground. Getting punched directly on the nose quickly made such feelings surface, even when you retaliated.

And sometimes a teacher would make a comment that hurt, especially if you liked the teacher and admired a little lady within hearing distance who thought you were "the berries."

But even youngsters turned 10-going-on-20 had to show their true feelings once in a while. The strain would otherwise be unbearable.

Home was the place where you put your facade aside. There, you found out that a few good yells seemed to reduce the severity of corporal punishment, which was not unusual in my growing-up days. The louder the ouches, the quicker my mother would arrive on the scene and attempt to bring the punishment to a halt.

It was different when you lost face at home than with your peers at school. They knew more about you at home since they were there when you first arrived on earth. You didn't have to prove anything to them. They expected you to cry if you were hurt or badly disappointed.

Home was about the only permissible place to cry and even then, you didn't want to overdo the bit because you didn't want to think of yourself as a cry baby.

A YOUNGSTER HAS a different view of the world and people.

For one thing, he believes being brave means not being afraid. If he is afraid of something, he thinks it makes him a coward and that is the last thing on earth he wants to be.

His role models are one-dimensional. He knows his father is not afraid of anything or anyone and has never shed a tear because he is a real man.

And the heroes he sees on the silver screen, most of them were cowboys back then, certainly never cry and hardly ever show any emotion of any kind, or acting ability.

In fact they very seldom kiss the ladies. This is one of his weaknesses, and he is going to have to work on this weakness if he wants to be a real man like Tom Mix or Tim McCoy.

And I'll bet a big sports hero like Babe Ruth and Lou Gehrig never cried, no matter what. Must have been a bunch of namby-pamby adults in the movie audience on the separate occasions when these two legends of baseball said their farewells to their baseball fans. Otherwise why would so-called grown people, especially "real men," keep dabbing at their eyes?

The two greats were not just bidding goodbye to the game they loved, but to the world which idolized them. They were dying.

I WAS 13 when my tonsils and adenoids were removed. Everything went well until a couple of days later when I decided to get out of bed and play ball.

A hemorrhage followed and I was rushed to the hospital that night. There was trouble stopping the flow of blood and my parents were very worried about me.

When I regained consciousness, I looked up and saw my mother and father. I expected my mother to be concerned as she tried to smile through her tears.

My father was more reserved. Up to that point I had never seen him cry. But he was crying as I opened my eyes and looked up at him.

I never knew my father had ever cried. It was years until I ever saw him shed tears again. But from that moment on I saw my father in a different light.

I saw a "real man" who was also a vulnerable human being. Real men did cry sometimes. And I realized that just because he wasn't demonstrative, it didn't mean he didn't love me.

My eyes had been opened somewhat. I was growing up.

YET, I MADE SURE I didn't cry at my father's funeral. I felt like it time and again, but I was not going to cry in front of others.

I held back so long, it became painful. On the way home I couldn't cry. I asked myself what was wrong with me. Why wasn't I crying over my father's death?

That night as I lay sleeplessly in bed, a torrential rainstorm came down. The actuality and the symbolism of the water seeping into the freshly dug cold ground, broke the dam of my uncried tears.

A flood of tears and regrets poured out as I grieved for my father.

The boy had finally become a "real man."

I Told You
I Hate Goodbyes

ALL OF US DO SOME THINGS better than others. And saying goodbye is not one of the things I do well.

No matter how hard I try — and I've had many years of practice — there is a tentativeness, an uneasy stirring of emotion when it comes to "goodbye."

Now I can say "hello" with the best of 'em. I say "hello" with conviction, ease and authority and if I say it as if I mean it, it's because I do.

I'm emphatic and positive with "hello." I like helloing people. I dislike goodbyes and my dislike for goodbye increases in direct proportion to my liking for the person.

It has always been that way with me. I can vividly recall the sadness of a youngster telling his mother goodbye as he left to attend the first day of school.

This was many years ago, but the feeling of leaving behind a shield of loving protectiveness for an unknown and possibly hostile world, that I will never forget.

I recall telling my parents goodbye on leaving for my first camping experience. Strangely, it occurs even to a kid how much more important his parents appear to him when he is about to leave them, even if it is for just a couple of weeks.

And how fine it was to get back home, even after having a

great adventuresome time at camp. Everything looked just right and reassuring, especially my parents. The familiarity that had been taken for granted was now seen as a rock, a foundation, a stabilizing influence that could be counted on.

It was early in life that I began saying "hello" with feeling and conviction. It was because I meant it.

LEAVING FOR THE ARMY is a definitive way of finding out that parting is sweet sorrow. There are parents who are worried about you and there is the unknown that the soldier is worried about.

And during wartime when a soldier leaves for overseas, his goodbyes take on a special significance. Wives and children hate goodbyes as much as the soldier.

The unspoken thought looms even bigger: "Will I see them again?" and "When?"

There is a lot of stiff-upper-lipping on these occasions and no one really fools anyone even though tears have been temporarily fought back and smiles have tried to hide the pain and fear.

I recall trying to place a call to my wife just before going overseas. The telephone lines were overburdened with just such and other calls, and when one finally reached his party, a dear voice could just barely be heard over the crackling and popping noises that were part of long distance calling back then.

At such a time it was difficult for either party to have a smiling voice.

More often than not the words rushed together. This was no time for small talk. The words "I love you" were the most important words in the English language. Even if the rest of the conversation was garbled and somewhat unintelligible, the purpose of the call had been accomplished.

Each branch of the service had its own spine-tingling battle song, but the universal refrain of "I love you, too" heard on that old phone was the real song that inspired the soldier and enabled him to face what was ahead.

THE FIRST TIME a child leaves home for an extended stay is the first real test for a parent to say "goodbye" while smiling and seemingly unconcerned.

At college age, the tables have turned. The youngster is more likely delighted to leave the hearth and home and be on his own, away from the supervision of old-fogey parents whose ideas seem to come from another planet.

By this time, Junior or Sis have learned how to overcome homesickness and loneliness. Camps and out-of-town trips to Aunt Beatrice and Uncle Arthur have taught them confidence and reliance.

But their parents have learned to become somewhat attached to these sometimes complex and difficult young individuals.

The many years of living have acquainted them with the potholes ahead. They would like to keep their kids from making some of the same mistakes, but they know they are no longer in the driver's seat. And away from home, the youngsters will be especially vulnerable.

But you let them go because that is the thing to do. How else will they become good, skillful "drivers" who can successfully negotiate life's highways?

HE WAS THE FIRSTBORN and the first to go off to college. His mother and I were doing fine as we helped him get his luggage into his Nashville dormitory, and his mother remade his bed and gave him some last-minute housekeeping advice.

"Don't worry, Mom," he kept saying. He seemed to be a picture of poise and confidence. "I'll be just fine."

It was finally time to leave. "I'll walk you to the car," he told us.

We chatted as he walked with his arm around his mother's shoulder. She used this brief opportunity to give him a couple of dozen more "do's" and "don't's" and he smiled tolerantly.

His father gave him a couple of pep-talk sentences, including "I know you'll do fine" and "drop us a line once in a while."

His mother added, "Call us if you feel like it."

We embraced our son before we got into our car. We were proud of him as we are our other two children. But he was the first to go off to school.

"Take good care of yourself," his mother said with a big brave smile. "Goodbye," and we started back home, this time without our son. He began walking back to his dormitory.

"Now that wasn't too bad," I told my wife as we drove off. Me and my big mouth. Up to then my wife had managed to be the soul of bravery. And then she looked back and our son had also turned to look back.

That was all it took to bring on a flood of tears.

"He's so all alone," said my wife, dabbing at her eyes with a handkerchief. "That's our baby we're leaving."

"Some baby," I said. "Look how big and tall he is. He'll be just fine."

"You know what I mean," said Betty, as she kept waving at our son until he was out of sight.

I knew exactly what she meant. I didn't need a handkerchief because it wouldn't help a lump in my throat.

He was the first one that left home. Then there would be others.

The goodbyes never got much easier.

TRAIN STATIONS WERE ONCE the scene of numerous farewells. Now it is the airport terminal where the traveler is bade "good luck" and "come back soon."

Look around and see and feel the mixture of excitement, sadness and drama of those who leave and those who are left.

When Banny, Betty's mother, arrived, it was always a joyous occasion to go to the airport. She was a pleasure to be around. She loved life and people and her enthusiasm was contagious.

But as the years went by, Banny needed help getting on and off the big planes that brought her to and from Florida.

And each time when she told us "goodbye" there would be more emotion in her voice.

The last time she asked us, "Will I ever see you again?"

That particular goodbye was a rough one on all of us. Banny looked vulnerable as she smiled that beautiful smile of hers.

We saw her again sometime later, but it was in a Florida hospital. It was our last goodbye to Banny. This time there would not be a "hello."

TELLING MY DAUGHTER goodbye is one of the toughest goodbyes of all.

Every once in a while she drives home to see us. The drive is a grueling one, since she lives in Memphis. But she is young and the drive doesn't take its toll on her as it does on us, especially in bad weather. So she doesn't wait for us.

The few wonderful days she spends go in a great hurry and then it is time to say goodbye.

Even hours before she is ready to leave for her trip back to Memphis, I get an edgy feeling. After her mother has kissed her goodbye, and exchanged "I love you's," I usually follow her to a service station down the road to make certain her car checks out and her fuel, oil and tires are okay. Wonder how she gets by without me when I'm not around?

But you can't prolong the going away past a certain point. The stalling has bought me a few more minutes but the pain of parting is always there.

"Goodbye honey, drive carefully. I love you."

"Goodbye Daddy. I love you and Mom."

She waves and that pretty face smiles as she drives off and I hurt like the dickens. I do it every time. It gets worse with each parting.

And the sadness of the parting often lasts for hours. It depresses me.

"You shouldn't let it get to you like that," my wife says.

I've tried to analyze my feelings. The only thing I can arrive at is:

Each "goodbye" is a one-way ticket. There is no round-trip ticket guarantee.

I told you I hate good-byes.

You Are Not
That Same Person

THE YOUNG HUSBAND AND WIFE were having marital problems. They love each other but they were beginning not to like each other. And being two people who still believed that marriage is not just a prelude to divorce, they wanted to do something about the situation before it got worse

So they did what isn't done very often these days. They called on a trusted older friend of the family and put their cards on the table, face up.

They knew he would be objective and wouldn't point an unfair finger of blame at either of them. They also knew he had been around long enough to pick up a few pointers about life and marriage.

So, they made an "appointment" with their friend who had blocked out whatever time they needed on a Saturday afternoon when his office is normally closed.

Did any of their problems arise because either had strayed or lost interest in each other?

"Absolutely not," said the husband. "I guess we're old fash-ioned in that and other ways." No, that definitely wasn't an issue.

He said they had a long, frank discussion with the older man as a husband and wife tried to explain what was bugging them.

"TOO MUCH TIME at the office, and often on weekends," was one of the wife's complaints. "Not enough time with me and the children."

Also she recalled how he once liked to dance and go to parties and how that is now low or almost non-existent on his list of priorities.

The husband said his wife didn't seem to be as interested in what he is doing as she once was.

"She now is more interested in her own career and clubs and hobbies. Her mother does most of the child managing."

So went the informal and non-recriminatory discussion, with the older friend doing more listening than talking.

"He just let us air our grievances. There were more things that we talked about, such as our different tastes in television programs, books and even friends."

He said the "counselor" listened and did a lot of smiling and nodding and that "when the conference was over, I think we had the answer to our so-called problems before our friend said a word.

"We knew that our marriage was in much better shape than most marriages and that we were luckier than we had realized."

The definitive complaint was:

"He's not the same person I married."

"She's not the same person I married."

They were both right, and during their candid give-and-take they realized this was the case even before their friend said:

"You are both absolutely right. And as long as you realize this and allow for the changes that take place, you'll get along just fine. Your marriage will last the way you want it to."

The husband said, "It seems strange, but it took a conference with a third party, a friend, for us to realize we had changed and were different from the people who married 10 years ago.

"We were different, but we weren't allowing for the changes

that had taken place. We are different people now, but if we still have the same feelings for each other, we'll be able to adjust and accommodate and get along just fine, just as our friend said."

I DON'T KNOW too many people who like change just for the sake of change. Most people, including myself, want a good reason for change. Most of us like the security and comfort of the known, especially if what we have is good, or not too bad.

And yet there are some changes that are inevitable. Changes take place all around us. Our environment changes and we change molecularly and emotionally day to day.

The changes that take place on a yearly basis would surprise us if we listed them one by one.

Our way of looking at life, our interests and drives, our priorities, all these change during our lifetime. Sometimes the difference is barely perceptible. In other instances it is very noticeable.

MANY HUSBANDS do get caught up in the sometimes exciting competition of making a living or a fortune, to the extent that wife and family take a backseat.

Yet, in this age of two working parents per family, many wives are doing the same thing.

That cute little bride is now a hard-driving career lady. She no longer hangs on to her husband's every word. She, too, has outside interests and sometimes even the children must take a backseat to those interests. It's a different world.

Meanwhile, that slim, handsome guy with the wavy hair is many pounds heavier and many hairs thinner.

The little bride no longer has the innocent, wide-eyed look of a Hollywood ingenue, but she is still pretty in his eyes, if he loves her.

And she feels the same way about that overweight ex-athlete, if she still loves him. To her, he is still handsome. Love produces astigmatisms.

Physical changes and changes brought about through time and circumstance will continue throughout life. All sorts of changes will continue. The way we perceive life and our mates and even ourselves will also change.

The only real constant on this earth is to remain steadfastly in love with each other. That is the only thing we can depend on if two people so will it.

PEOPLE ARE BOUND to make mistakes. They sometimes marry for the wrong reasons and they often divorce for the wrong reasons.

The guy who marries the "prettiest girl in school" because she is the prettiest, is heading for disappointment down the road.

Unless she is unusually enduring, those looks will fade somewhat. Springtime becomes summer and then fall, and then other factors — her character, her pleasant disposition, her concern, her love for you — will become of prime importance.

There must be other reasons than physical beauty for a marriage to have taken place and for it to hold together. Looks are fleeting. They change.

There is nothing more pathetic than the one-dimensional woman who feels that when she is no longer as pretty as a picture, that she is literally out of the picture.

It is also sad for her husband to put so much emphasis on the physical side of their relationship that once her beauty fades, he feels he has in a sense been betrayed. Actually, he is the one who is doing the betraying. He has not considered the total person.

A MARRIAGE CAN SUFFER because of lack of concern and affection. But it also needs space and room for both parties to grow.

Marriage is like two ships at sea accompanying each other side by side for the long voyage ahead. In that way they can offer each other protection in case of danger and avert disaster. But they need enough room between them for each ship to react to the swell and fall of the waves and the tide.

As close as they are, they are individual ships with individual needs. If they were lashed together, they would shred and splinter each other from the separate reactions they have to the action of the sea.

The businessman "counselor" gave the young couple this analogy when he was advising them at his office. He stressed the need for each partner to respect the other and to allow for the partner's highs and lows.

He also reminded them they are different now than when their marriage was launched on the sea of matrimony.

BREATHING IS ALSO
DULL AND ROUTINE

I'LL HAVE TO ADMIT my wife and I have become used to a sizable amount of routine and structure in our lives and that rather than making us restless and discontent, it usually has the opposite effect.

Certainly, every now and then we like a change of pace to add an additional dash of spice and excitement, but on a week-to-week basis, we like the routine of work and reuniting at home and the informal resting up or occasionally going out on Sundays.

But this past weekend was different. Betty complained she was not feeling well on Friday, and I heeded because she does not cry wolf.

Saturday and Sunday were very untypical for this bundle of energy. She spent most of each day in bed.

Our doctor tells us we are good patients but not-so-good customers because he seldom hears from us. We have been lucky that way and in many other ways.

Both of us hesitate to call a doctor unless it is a dire emergency. We try the drug store first. But this time the medicine that was supposed to help a stomach virus didn't help.

Finally Betty said, "Maybe we should call the doctor." She was in excruciating pain and nothing seemed to help.

I phoned our doctor and he told me to bring her to the

hospital. She was shocked at the sudden turn of events. Hospitals are not her favorite places. But this was different. She could hardly move, but we finally got there.

VARIOUS TESTS DIDN'T reveal what was wrong. "But something is going on and you should be admitted," said the emergency room doctor.

"What a way to spend a Sunday," Betty tried to quip. Yes, the doctor thought the trip was necessary.

So did our family physician when he saw how much pain Betty was experiencing in her abdominal region. "You may have to be operated on tonight, but let's see what the surgeon says."

The surgeon emphatically agreed. "I don't know what is wrong but something needs to be attended to immediately. Frankly, I don't know what we are operating for, but we'll find out."

Would medication help? I always thought when an operation was indicated that two opinions were better than one. But there was such a note of urgency in the doctors' voices I felt this was not the time for another opinion. Life often puts us on spots requiring flexibility and rethinking. "What do you think?" asked my wife. "You're the one in pain," I said not unsympathetically.

It isn't easy to tell a doctor to start cutting on your wife of 42 years for an exploratory operation.

We both agreed the operation seemed necessary. There was too much pain. Something was seriously wrong.

The surgeon assured me and our son he would keep us posted. In just a matter of moments, they were wheeling Betty toward the operating room. What a change from the usual Sunday routine we enjoy.

The doctor was as good as his word. Within ninety minutes we were phoned three times about the progress of the operation.

"She is doing fine," we were told. "It was a ruptured appendix. We had to do a lot of housecleaning to get the poison out, but she is doing beautifully. She's lucky she didn't wait longer."

Thank God! I thought about the decision we had to make and about the dire consequences of not having the operation performed Sunday night. It would have been a game of Russian roulette, and we may have lost.

I was glad the doctors were insistent and didn't try to minimize the situation. I was grateful we were in the hands of these two fine doctors.

One never knows when you might need one of these truly dedicated savers of lives and salvagers of the happiness that exists between a husband and wife. I didn't need to be reminded of my good fortune.

But when they were wheeling my little lady away, brave smile, wave and all, I thought again how lucky I've been to have shared these many years with her. I gave her another kiss.

"She could get along without me much better than I could get along without her." My son understood, and so did his brother who came by a little later.

THE DESIGNATION "weaker sex" is a misnomer. Strength comes in various forms and packages. It isn't all measured by physical power. Faith and bravery play a big part.

"She is one tough little lady," the surgeon told us. "Her appendix probably ruptured Friday night. I'm amazed she could stand such pain until Sunday night."

And just a day before I hazarded the opinion my wife, who had been doing much moaning and groaning, "may have a low pain threshold." I apologize.

And there was the recovery period, made longer because of the offending appendix which wouldn't wait. Not too long ago, many such cases resulted in peritonitis and death. Now, modern medicine and antibiotics help patients to hang on and recover.

She never really was out of it. Even when she returned from the operation in a somewhat woozy condition, she reminded me to take out the garbage and to do a few important things around the house, including throwing away last week's TV schedule and not letting the papers accumulate.

She's a spunky little lady and I'll be glad to have her back home with me so we can get back into our routine which also includes just sitting near each other while we read or watch television.

Sometimes conversation isn't even necessary. We know how we feel.

Fate didn't have to prove to us how lucky we are. But the operation reaffirmed what we already knew.

Strange how history has a way of repeating itself. I didn't particularly like to be all alone when I was a kid. I didn't enjoy being home alone this past week. The nights were lonely. No one to talk or share the silence with.

The pop-up gear in the clothes drawer doesn't work. One takes for granted there are always clean shirts, socks and underwear when needed, until the replenisher isn't around and the cycle is broken.

Thank God we are back together. There is nothing dull about a routine you love, especially with the one you love.

A STOREHOUSE
FULL OF MEMORIES

IT'S AS IF A MAGNET draws me to the building.

At least once every two or three months, I'll change my usual route home and swing by Palmetto and Fifth for a "visit."

Sometimes I drive slowly and remember what the old structure means to me. On other occasions I park nearby and walk around the building where my parents had their first grocery store.

They are gone, but the building has stood its ground all of these many years — a lone sentinel since most of the other buildings and houses have been uprooted for parking lots.

And after such a visit with this former Mom and Pop grocery, I feel refreshed and revitalized. I have made contact with the past and with my parents.

Yet never on these visits had I gone inside the store, which has been remodeled several times, inside and out. It seemed to be enough for me to have this tangible link with the past. My own memories of how the busy little store looked were very real.

In my mind's eye, if I walked through the door, there would be numerous customers to be waited on by my mother and father. He, with the quick reflexes and wit. She, with the old-world heritage of not only standing by her man but working with him side-by-side.

And work they did. A forty-hour work week would have been considered a vacation. Saturday alone, the biggest day of the week, was easily a 19-hour day, by the time shelves were restocked and straightened.

I vividly recall such days. As a child I began waiting on customers in an era long before supermarkets. Each item, from a penny piece of candy to a dollar sack of flour, was presented to the customer by the clerk. WE were the clerks. There were no big shots.

Almost all of my teen-age years were connected with that busy little store, run by two people who not only understood free enterprise but appreciated a country that allowed them to work as long and as hard as they wanted to in order to fulfill a Mom and Pop American dream.

THIS WEEK I MADE another visit to the old building. But now there was more urgency. It was like not putting off a visit to a friend or relative who would soon be leaving.

This time the visit was a much longer one, and I also went inside the store, which is now called Scrappy's, a popular dining spot and watering hole for UTC students.

My parents' store had a personality of its own and was kept spotlessly clean. Scrappy's place has a different personality, but it is also clean and is a mood-setter for temporarily leaving cares behind.

Several diners were eating. A couple of customers were having a beer.

Unlike many years ago, no one was in that big a hurry to get waited on. There was a relaxed atmosphere. The only one moving fast was one of the young owners of the dining spot, who was in the kitchen area.

Several lamps and lighted signs flickered inside Scrappy's and something frying on the grill smelled nostalgically good. I could almost imagine that aroma coming from the little kitchen we had in the back of the store.

But even there, not much time was wasted refueling. The idea was to get something to eat and get back to work in a store that almost always seemed to be full of customers.

"Have you got a couple of minutes to spare?" I asked Joe Hannah, one of the owners of the restaurant and lounge.

"Sure," he said. "What can I do for you?"

I told him who I was and that my folks once ran a grocery store on this spot.

"Looks like we're both being dispossessed," I said.

"That's right," Joe agreed. "The university is buying my property and I'll be out of business after the first of the new year."

Then the building will be torn down. Many of the mansions and hovels of the area have long ago bitten the dust.

SCRAPPY'S SITS ON a small lot and is one of five parcels the university has acquired or is in the process of purchasing. Joe said he received a "fair price" but would rather not have sold because of the prime location.

"But things change," Joe said. He will try to find another location near the campus, but there aren't too many left.

This land, plus property on which UTC's old physical plant is located, will be used to build new student housing.

It's the old story of the old making way for the new. "I suppose you can't stop progress," Joe said.

After my visit inside with Joe, I went outside and walked around the once thriving grocery store. There are still a few houses behind the business and I could almost see people sitting on the porches and calling their kids to come in.

I could almost hear the zing of rocks whizzing by my ears.

Rock-throwing was a popular pastime for the youths of that day.

So was eating groceries, and we sold tons of food at the store on Palmetto and Fifth.

FOR A FEW YEARS we lived in rooms on top of that old building.

I remember it was cold much of the time during winter. The heat in summertime didn't seem to bother me.

What did get to me was my mother's insistence that I practice on my violin at least an hour each day. I was not cut out to be a violinist, but no one could convince my mother I didn't have some great hidden talent.

In order to be set free for a couple of hours to play my kind of playing, I would place my violin on a bed, read a Tom Swift or pirate book and saw away at the poor instrument.

The fact my folks couldn't tell the difference between these sounds and the caterwauling that came when I had the instrument under my chin, clues you in on the caliber of my musicianship.

I CAN STILL SEE my playmate, Ed, eating sardines in the little kitchen. I had swapped him King Arthur for Possum sardines because he was eating Possum sardines with such gusto and he didn't mind swapping.

Of course, Ed was always hungry and almost anything tasted good to him. Ed was also very street-wise.

Our grocery store was sort of a style setter with students who went to East Fifth Street School. There would be periods of dill pickle popularity, followed by ice cream cones dipped in hot chocolate.

The store brings back memories of customers who were real characters and of Uncle Sid who was unique. He was a part-time clerk and all-around helper and trouble shooter.

"What is to be, will be," opined Uncle Sid, "and what ain't to be might accidentally happen." Thus summing up the unpredictability of life.

But the driving force in the store was my Dad. He was a combination of good, honest businessman with a heart and a terrific sense of humor.

He once weighed an unsophisticated customer piecemeal. "Give me your arm, now your other arm, now your head, now your leg and the other leg."

This was done on a counter scale that only pulled 30 pounds. But his guesstimate was 185, causing the customer to exclaim:

"I done lost two pounds since last week."

My mother wondered why my Dad took time out for such shenanigans, but that was exactly what he was doing. Time out for fun. Everyone in the crowded store enjoyed it including the weighee.

THEY'LL BE TEARING DOWN that old store very soon. You can't hang on to something forever.

The owners of Scrappy's will be giving up a thriving business. I'm losing a tangible connection with my past, and it hurts.

Ask Betty, who can no longer point out where progress obliterated her parents' store many years ago.

Neither of my parents attended college, but they were well versed in the meaning of ethics, free enterprise, citizenship and family and civic values.

They never received an honorary degree, but maybe the University of Tennessee at Chattanooga could put up a modest plaque where the building will be torn down. It's now aptly named Scrappy's, in honor of a scrappy coach.

The plaque might simply state:

"On this site, Sam and Mary Parker proved that the principles of their beloved, adopted country worked.

"The principles worked because these two proud citizens were given the God-given freedom and opportunity to work and dream at the site of this Mom and Pop grocery opened in the year 1919."

The 'Guarantee' And The Freight Train

"I THINK WE ARE ALL better off not knowing what is waiting for us down the road. I think it's good that we don't know how long we're going to be here and how we're going to leave."

"I don't know about that," said a more pragmatic individual in our group. "If I had a definite timetable, knew exactly how long I was going to stick around, I think that would give me the edge."

He said he could better plan his life and utilize his time.

"I believe it would make me more conscious of each day and would keep me from squandering time the way most of us do."

Another one said, "Knowing when I was going to that big city room in the sky would make me more conscious all right. But I think it would be in a negative sort of way.

"Every day I'd remind myself that on a given day, month, and year I would leave this planet Earth. I think I'd spend too much time worrying about it and not enough time making the best of each day."

He said he was glad "we don't have a definite timetable. I believe it's for the best."

"I think you're right," said another member of the group. "Knowing we are mortal is one thing, but knowing the date and nature of our mortality is something else. This knowledge alone would make us uptight.

"Let me ask you a hypothetical question: Suppose there was such a thing as a guarantee that you would live to be 99 years old and that they would be 99 reasonably happy and healthy years. And there was also a stipulation that sometime during the last year, the 99th, you would cash in by being hit by a freight train. Would you opt for that guarantee?"

THERE WAS A PAUSE and then someone asked: "What made you think of something that far out?"

"I was just trying to make a point," said the poser of the hypothetical and philosophical question. It was his contention that even though the person knew that he would live much longer than the average life span, the certainty of being hit by a train at age 99 "would cause him to spend a lifetime of worry about being hit by a train."

How many in the group of five would take the "guarantee" and the crunching consequence?

One said he would. "The way things are going now," he said, "I'd be lucky to live until I'm 70. Sure, I'd take a 99-year guarantee, and then I'd stay away from the railroad tracks."

On a more serious note, I believe the Deity in His infinite wisdom has done us a great favor by not giving us a "D" Day (D is for Departure) from the date of our birth.

Unlike other living species, we understand the tenuousness of the strand of life. Somewhere as the years go by it occurs to us to do as much with our lives as possible on a day-to-day basis.

By not, to our knowledge, being assigned an exit date ahead of time, we are able to hope from one day to the next. And that is one unbelievably immense gift!

It is what keeps most of us going when there doesn't seem to be any way out of a situation. It is what makes us hold on to life even when there is pain and grief. Tomorrow may be better.

Hope is truly one of the greatest gifts mankind has received. That's why I don't want to know when that "freight train" is going to do me in — with or without a hypothetical "guarantee."

'Starting Over' On A Day-To-Day Basis

"If I had to do it all over again," he said, "I'd do a lot of things differently."

Wouldn't we all if we had the hindsight of experience to back us up. But chances are, if we started from scratch, we'd probably make the same mistakes all over again. Most of us learn our most valuable lessons the hard way . . . by trial and error.

Which brings me to a friend's theory for "starting over" and thereby cashing in on what he has already learned from experience.

He said, "Each time I hear someone say he wishes he had the chance to start all over again, I say he has that chance if he means it. Of course we won't be given the chance for a completely new start, but we can give ourselves that chance on a day-to-day basis."

He said he had been "starting over" every day since he realized the value of his theory, which he described as "so simple and effective it makes me wonder why everyone doesn't use it."

As with so many insights and discoveries, his theory evolved over a period of time on a step-to-step basis.

"I'm one of those people," he said, "who got an enormous satisfaction in welcoming in the new year. It gave me a fresh start. It was a new beginning, sort of like having a shiny new car without any scratches or dents."

He said he enjoyed ringing in the New Year so much he began analyzing why he got "such a charge" from this ritual, a new beginning which was "almost like a religious experience."

WHAT HE CAME UP WITH was this:

"It's like being forgiven for the mistakes I had made and I had been given a new year to do better. Sometimes I made resolutions which I wrote down, but most of the time I just kept them in my head."

His "theory" began germinating when in very human fashion he broke most of his resolutions before March or April of the new year.

"I'd feel like I'd let myself down and would have to wait for another year to start all over again."

But why wait that long? Why not use his next birthday as another beginning? Why not, indeed, and then:

"It hit me that every day the sun sets and rises is another opportunity for me to make a fresh start. The sum total of my experience can be used to make the next day the most successful day I ever lived."

Now he doesn't have to wait for a full year to go by in order to be forgiven for past mistakes and to make amends. He now does this on a daily basis.

Another beautiful aspect of his day-to-day "starting over" is that he forgives himself for past blunders. "This is more important than it may seem. It works for me and lets me start out with a clean slate each day.

"I find I don't get bogged down by my regrets, self-recriminations and feelings of guilt. Why hang on to that extra weight if you can get rid of it?"

HIS THEORY SEEMS to serve him well, and I was curious to know some of the changes he had made or would like to make if they weren't too personal.

"No problem," he assured me. "Most of the changes I want to make are far from world-shaking or even dramatic, but they are things I think are needed for me to live a more fulfilling life."

He said one thing he has worked on each day "is to try to make each day count for something. Too many people seem to take each day for granted. They get up in the morning and drag to work and very often their whole day is a drag.

"They lack the enthusiasm and excitement that will help make the day a success for themselves and for others. Then they wonder why people don't crowd around them."

Somewhere along the line he determined he was going to "get the most out of each day."

This ties in with his zest for work and for living. His theory of daily clean-slate fresh starts neatly dovetails with his determination not to let the mistakes, bitterness, self-recrimination and guilt of yesterday "spill over and ruin today."

OF COURSE THERE WERE numerous personal changes he had made in his life. Changes that gradually took place and made a big difference for him and for his wife.

One which he could share had to do with "quality time" with his family.

"Some years ago it hit me that providing for my family was just a part of being a husband and a father. I also needed to provide more time with my family

"This revelation, which I wish had come earlier, has added an important dimension to my life, one which I treasure."

His experience has also taught him the value of priorities.

Things that once seemed to have the highest priorities considerably dropped in importance. "Each day," he said, "I am reminded of the miracle of waking up another day and being relatively free of pain.

"Ask someone who hardly knows an hour free of pain and that person will tell you about priorities; what is and isn't important."

A CHANGE HE HAS worked over a period of many years: "To be less critical of others and try to understand what makes them tick."

Equally as important, in his estimation, is "to be less critical of myself. It has at last dawned on me that I should strive for perfection but not to be too upset when it isn't achieved."

Here is another breakthrough in his thinking which he regards as a very important change for him:

"It took me a long time to realize that others don't perceive us as we perceive ourselves and it is true the other way around.

"I was constantly being hurt because I expected others to think and feel the way I did, but that is often not the case."

Even husbands and wives should "allow for the fact they are seeing certain situations from different points of view. As close as they are, they're individuals with individual feelings and perceptions." He realizes his "starting over each day" theory isn't perfect because "there are some chances you'll never have again."

He said, "You might now be a different, more tolerant, patient and understanding sort of parent, but those youngsters have grown up and have kids of their own. That's the kind of chance you won't get again unless you're young enough."

However, there are many opportunities every day "to bring about some good changes in your life."

OTHER CHANGES he has brought about:

Having more friends "from various strata" of society. "This makes for a fuller life."

Being more generous with deserving praise in person, by phone or in a note.

Being more tolerant of those he comes in contact with and not overlooking their strengths and talents because of their weaknesses.

He emphasized the "ultimate change" is the constant change taking place in our lives and in the world.

He said, "Change is constant and the sooner we get used to the idea, the better we can ride with the punches. Some people burn out early because they can't adapt to changes in their lives.

"We change, our thinking changes, and how we feel about people and they in turn about us, this also changes."

He said,"One of the best changes I ever made in my life was to wake up to the fact that everything changes and not to be constantly in a state of surprise."

This goes back to his "day-to-day" theory.

A Family Member
Is Slipping Away

I HESITATED TO WRITE about our calico cat, CoCo.

After all there are many other subjects of more general interest. And besides, as difficult as we find it to understand, there are some people who just don't like cats.

For that matter, there are those who don't like dogs or any kind of pets or animals. There are also people who don't particularly like people.

But I decided to write about CoCo for several reasons. First, we dearly love this feisty, 13-year-old "lady," and secondly, we've been very worried about her lately because she is ill and her illness has cast a gloom on our household.

CoCo has hardly eaten a bite in the past two weeks. The last time she ate a tiny morsel, we were overjoyed. But now she shows no interest in food. This beautiful creature, an armful to lift not very long ago, has become as light as a little bundle of fluff.

Her luxuriously soft and "expensive" fur coat used to fit her perfectly. Now, she doesn't fill it out. It sort of hangs on her.

Seafood and chicken were her favorite foods. Now she shows no interest in any kind of food, and we have tried many different things to entice her. But she is literally starving.

"I wish," said Betty, "she could tell us what is bothering her.

She looks so sad and helpless. It's not like her at all. We've got to do something to help her."

So we took her to the animal hospital where she gets her annual shots. They kept her overnight for observation. It was the first time since she was a kitten that she had been away from home. It was also the first time since we married that my wife "felt all alone in the house."

She said, "Even when you weren't home, there were always the children around, and then we got CoCo. Just having her in the house was companionship. She was company."

I KNOW WHAT she means. Once when Betty was out of town for a few days, CoCo and I had some good conversations, although we didn't always agree.

There was something comforting about stroking her and feeling and hearing the gentle buzz of her contented purring.

And until she became ill, we had a routine that seldom varied. After I gave her food and water early in the morning, I would sit on the recliner with a cup of coffee in my hand. As soon as she heard the creak of the chair, she glided into the room and sat down beside me.

If I didn't pet her and scratch her head, she would let me know I wasn't doing one of the things I was put here on earth to do . . . to please her royal haughtiness.

So I'd sit for about five or 10 minutes, sip my coffee, pet her and generally get in the right frame of mind for another busy day.

Then it was time to brush and shave and she would wait, sometimes not too patiently, until she thought it was time for her to jump onto the sink. One of her favorite water sports was drinking water from the faucet. She also wanted to show off and prove she could jump like a coiled spring.

All of this has changed just in the past few weeks. The doctor at the animal hospital said he couldn't find any particular thing wrong with her.

"For one thing," he said, "she is old and maybe she is just running out of time." We winced when we heard this, although the thought had occurred to us.

He said UT has a veterinary college that might be able to determine what was ailing our cat. "They have more sophisticated and conclusive tests they can give her."

However, he agreed with us he "wouldn't put her through all that" because of her age. I also didn't want CoCo being experimented with.

He had given her a couple of shots to stimulate her appetite and told us to check back with him. She also didn't eat at the hospital.

OF COURSE EVERYONE believes their kids and pets are the smartest. That also goes for our cat.

CoCo seems to sense when we are going to put her in the cat carrier and she makes herself scarce. It has always been this way.

Even in her weakened condition, she struggled a little to prevent incarceration. But the struggle was pitifully weak and brief.

Usually when we bring her home from a visit to the doctor, she springs out of her cage, reorients herself and is back in business in a matter of minutes. She begins perking up even as we drive into the neighborhood she knows.

This time when we opened her cage she sat there for several minutes. And when she did decide to walk out it was on extremely wobbly legs.

She finally made it to the bedroom and sat down. "The old lady isn't feeling well."

"Yes," said my wife, "she just looks at you with those big eyes, and it breaks my heart not to be able to help her, especially if she's in pain."

I noticed our appetites were also diminished. After a light dinner we didn't talk much. We were depressed. Someone in our household was very sick.

The next day there was no early morning ritual that did me as much good as it did CoCo. I sat a few minutes on the recliner and sipped a cup of coffee, but she didn't show up to be petted. I felt I was missing something vital to my well-being.

After I shaved I didn't hear her "meow" indicating she wanted water from the faucet. So I lifted the light bundle of fur and waited to see if her pink tongue darted out at the running water. It has always been a game with her because she has water in a bowl which she usually ignores.

She also ignored the tiny amount of food I had given her. She didn't ask for it "by name" which she usually does.

"If she could only tell us what is bothering her. This is so pitiful and frustrating," said my wife.

I LEFT FOR WORK and a few hours later Betty went to her office.

A couple of hours into the workday, Betty called: "You know how she loves to jump up on the sink for water. Well I saw her try and almost make it. She got her front paws on the sink, but then she fell back down.

"I could have bawled. It was so pitiful. She's got so much spunk she tried again but this time she fell hard. I'm afraid she's going to hurt herself."

My wife said she lifted her on to the sink so she could "at least drink a little water since she won't eat anything."

Betty has called the veterinarian's office several times and she was told to bring CoCo in again if she doesn't do any better.

"Meanwhile she is in the house by herself. Should we ask Carrie to come by and keep an eye on her?"

Carrie is a friend of ours who helps Betty with the housework once a week. She is also a lady who loves people, cats and dogs. Carrie loves CoCo, and the feeling is reciprocated.

She brought along an eyedropper to see if she could coax some water and honey onto CoCo's tongue. She said she succeeded a couple of times and would "keep trying."

WE MAY HAVE TO leave her at the hospital again this weekend. We hope not. We're afraid if she goes back and doesn't improve, we may never see our beloved pet again.

It grieves us to see this vital and beautiful creature just dragging around the house. She has always gotten a lot out of life and given us even more in return. Now she sits and stares sadly.

Outside she had enjoyed her game of playing huntress, with the patience known only to a miniature lion as she stalked her prey. She also loved to sit on top of the carport surveying her domain and looking down haughtily at animals below her. Often she sat on the hood of my car. My wife said she thought she was "people."

Now our once big and feisty cat has been whittled down by age and whatever is bothering her, and it is sad for an animal lover to take.

Come on, you know what I'm talking about. Tell me YOU didn't shed some tears when that beloved pet of yours was very sick, and you heard the veterinarian say: "We might have to put her to sleep."

This was a "member" of your family he was talking about, not a stranger. This is someone you love and have become accustomed to and comfortable with. It isn't easy to think of life without CoCo. I tell you it hurts, and if this makes me a "softy," so be it.

Betty sees this soft tendency on our part as "something that makes us very human." People who "don't feel that way are missing something," she said.

I know HE has more important things to do, but I've prayed He'll make CoCo get well.

We love that spunky cat. Please get well, CoCo. We need you.

The World's Greatest Course For Parents

Does Someone Teach a Course in Parenting?

Yes. Listen to the memories of your own childhood.

Think back and recall your feelings when you were unfairly treated by those in your little world, especially by your parents.

Recall the guilt and even shame when you were told you weren't as smart as Johnny down the street who invariably made all "A's" but who couldn't throw a ball half as far as you could. Remember how it felt to feel stupid whether the word was used or implied and you were seldom able to "do anything right."

Remember the frustration of never being able to make a decision on your own, although some of your decisions would have gotten you into deep trouble.

Recall the fear of the other shoe dropping and always being at the mercy of someone, including your parents. All the more reason for you to show more tolerance and mercy for your youngsters.

Can you recall how important it was for you to please your parents, especially your father who at times acted as if you didn't exist? And when he did notice you it was to cuff you a couple of times for what he considered was improper behavior?

There are grown men who go through life hurting for the

affection and approval they didn't get from their parents, especially from their fathers. Their own interests are sublimated in the desire to gain the approval and respect of "the old man."

Actually, they may be seeking a parental love that was not apparent enough in their formative years. Too many parents take for granted their children know they love them.

Children feel what they see and hear. Nuances are often lost on them. Sometimes they need a hug, a pat, a kiss or a loving and reassuring word.

YOU HEAR MUCH ABOUT the drug scene and peer pressure, but peer pressure is nothing new. It has always been around, only now there is pressure to follow in the footsteps of those who get into even more serious trouble.

But why do some kids feel so overwhelmed they think they are literally at the end of their rope, as if there is no tomorrow?

Here again, if parents will try to remember their own feelings and frustrations in their childhood, it will help them cope with children who are seemingly unable to cope.

I believe it is lack of perspective and experience that makes some young people feel their life isn't worth living.

If you've been around for a goodly number of years, you realize the ebb and flow of life is just that. When you think you are riding high, you are likely to have the rug pulled out from under you.

When you have fallen flat on your face and there appears no way of getting off the floor, dusting yourself off and looking the world in the eye, you have enough perspective to realize things can and do change. Tomorrow is another day and another opportunity. You may very well ride high again.

The young haven't been around long enough to experience

this cycle of success and failure. Each defeat and disappointment becomes a major calamity from which they feel there is no recovery.

This is where communication is vitally important. Parents can assure the young there is always tomorrow. They've been there. Parents and children should communicate more.

"I can't live without him" is a sincerely expressed lament. It comes from a broken heart, and make no mistake, young feelings are important.

But parents know you can recover from some of life's most cruel and staggering blows and that life goes on, and should go on.

It is too precious for anyone to extinguish, especially a young, unfulfilled life full of promise and the chance to be a good parent to children of one's own.

YOU SAY YOUR CHILDHOOD wasn't an idyllic case of joyful and genteel upbringing and that it has left some scars. Join the multitude who understand a situation in which firmness almost resembles cruelty.

But you are now an enlightened parent who realizes one can often learn more from negative situations than from good ones.

You aren't about to cop out and use the excuse you are locked into negative parental behavior because you are only doing what you were taught to do by your parents. You have learned from their constructive efforts as well as from their mistakes.

You have also learned the importance of not holding a grudge against them for their transgressions nor against yourself. This is not good for you nor for them. They thought they were doing a good job, and the best they could do, long before the science of parenting was given very much thought.

Let this be the guideline for yourself and other enlightened parents:

Treat your children the way you would have liked to have been treated as a child.

Does someone teach a course in parenting?

Yes. Listen to the memories of your own childhood.

A 'Prisoner' In
His Own Home

I'VE ALWAYS BEEN an exercise nut. Long before this current exercise craze, I stuck to an exercise regimen that I felt kept me in better-than-average shape.

Whether I went about it in a scientific manner is up for debate, but it worked for me. It made me feel better and that is basically what counts.

Over the years I've grudgingly eased up and my workouts have become a little less rigorous. Let's not fib. They are a lot less rigorous than they were, say, five years ago when I was still exercising with barbells.

But there are certain things a compulsive exerciser won't give up, certain free-swinging arm and leg exercises that I once warmed up with before I began my workout with weights about twice a week.

Now I do these rigorously, sometimes thinking about those cold weights downstairs that I haven't lifted in several years. Maybe I'll still go back to them. Just cut down on their poundage — and mine.

So there I was exercising in another part of the house. I was coming down to the last leg of my 30-minute workout. Now for the ten side-straddle hops.

"...seven, eight, nine, ouch, %%##!!!......wow, that smarts."

I yelled loud and clear. My wife heard me at the other end of the house.

"What's the matter?"

"I must have pulled a muscle or a ligament. I heard something snap. It hurts and burns like uh, ...the devil. Wish I had stopped on eight instead of nine."

BY NOW MY WIFE was in my room. "I don't know why you have to do that jumping exercise where both of your feet leave the ground at the same time."

"Because that's the way it's done and that's the way I've been doing it for more than 50 years. I must not have been concentrating. That's why I hurt myself."

My wife suggested I put some ice on it right away. I told her it wasn't that big a deal.

The next day I could hardly walk and agreed to have her and our daughter drive me to the doctor's office.

"You should have put something cold on it as soon as you hurt yourself. Your knee would have been better by now," said the doctor.

"Now, you'll need heat and this pain reliever, this knee brace and these crutches. And stay off your feet for at least ten days. The x-ray doesn't indicate anything broken. But if you don't take it easy your knee could need operating on."

To my wife's credit, she didn't say a word about recommending the ice treatment. But there was a faint flicker of a smile. I knew what she was thinking.

She had the same sort of smile when she asked me after my pulled-ligament accident:

"Didn't you feel good before you exercised?"

"Yeah. Why?"

"Then why did you exercise?"

It's tough to argue with a woman's pragmatic logic.

"Naturally I exercised because it makes me feel better."

"Do you feel better now?" asked my wife.

"Now don't start up with me," I said as good-naturedly as I knew how.

What she said didn't get to me as much as that patronizing look which in effect said: "There, there, I know how it is with you little boys who refuse to slow up."

I think it said "slow up," not "grow up."

I think that look also asked: "What are you trying to prove after all of these years?"

But maybe what I'm trying to prove is what keeps me going. Who knows?

SO THERE I SAT on my recliner after I got back from the doctor's office.

For a couple of days I used that ugly, unwieldy leg brace which went over my trousers and resembled something worn by a goalie at a hockey game.

I tried my crutches, but each step jolted me and caused me to teeter and I figured the doctor didn't need any more business from me. Besides, the powerful pain and ligament medicine made me even more unsteady.

But to my credit, for a guy who likes to be mobile, I did sit there for hours on end with my foot propped up as prescribed as I watched hour after hour of television, read a little from this and that book and looked at magazines and then back at the television set.

Even programs that I formerly liked became hateful and boring. The commercials were especially driving me nuts with their lack of restraint and appeal to the lowest possible denominator. Even more than the programs they shrieked of poor taste.

Answering a phone was a major operation. Putting on a pair of socks and shoes was a juggling act. All because of one lousy knee, I was literally out of commission. Out of whack and sync with society. I didn't feel like shaving and I didn't.

This was no vacation. It was painful captivity. I was feeling extremely vulnerable. And when my boys and the grandchildren came to see me, I was busy worrying about whether my knee would be accidentally kicked or maybe on purpose. So much so that I didn't enjoy them as much as usual.

My knee was hurting me, physically, psychologically and emotionally. I wanted out of that "easy" chair. I wanted to go back to work. I wanted to feel useful again.

If you get the idea I was feeling sorry for myself, you're right. I was. "Wish I had quit on eight and had concentrated a little more."

FLIPPING CHANNELS, I came across the Boston Marathon. By far, the most gripping event was the race by the wheelchair athletes held in conjunction with the marathon.

The streets were rain-slippery and these daring athletes on their very light, race-adapted wheelchairs were not holding back.

There was more than prize money involved. There was the pride and the competitiveness of the race watched by millions of people throughout the world.

I have been touched by these gallant people in previous races. This time they got to me even more. They were inspiring.

Perhaps sitting there temporarily crippled caused me to better relate and empathize and to comprehend in a small measure the odds they faced and their undaunted spirit which beat the odds on that rain-swept day.

Muscular arms pumped furiously and the wheelchairs hurled down the sloping street. At the outset they were bunched together, and I was afraid of what might happen. And happen it did.

Wheelchair after wheelchair collided and hurled the already broken bodies of the athletes on to the street. Some were bruised and shaken. Others were stunned and more badly hurt. But somehow, each athlete was lifted back on to his or her metal steed.

Arms of caring spectators carefully put them back on their chairs which allowed them to break the bonds which encircled half their bodies.

And then the powerful arms and even more powerful wills and spirits of these superior people began pumping again and it was all one could do to see the race clearly.

The closer I watched, the more blurred my vision became.

Who was I to feel sorry for myself? I felt like a jerk for the sympathy I had wasted on myself.

Life is full of twists and turns and accidents big and small. The wheelchair athletes I had been watching were bigger than life. They had conquered what life had dished out. And they were vigorously challenging it undaunted. They were the personification of the soaring, indomitable human spirit and will.

I looked at my propped-up hurt knee. Hopefully it would get better. My morale was better. I was humbled at what I had witnessed.

I WAS SUPPOSED TO "stay off" my feet for 10 days. Two days was all I could handle. Besides, I seem to be a fast healer and doctors are supposed to be conservative in their treatment and prognosis.

Getting in my car to go to work was tough. The hurt knee seemed to be telling me to take it easy, and what's the hurry and remember the doctor's warning.

But once I got in the car, it was worth it. This was my vehicle to freedom, to be able to get from this point to that point.

I was more aware than ever of the music of the engine and then the corny music on the radio which to my ears sounded better than a Carnegie Hall concert.

I was finally leaving that old "easy" chair and driving to a job that wasn't all that easy but a lot easier for me than just sitting there — a prisoner.

Life, it's wonderful. It needs to be lived to the fullest.

My knee? It's still protesting. But my morale tells it to pipe down and quit complaining.

INSIGHTS AND SMILES
HELP YOU GROW UP

WHEN I WAS A PRESCHOOLER, only three- or four-years-old at the time, the crow of a rooster stirred sad feelings of loneliness and displacement.

The feelings were intense and indelible though I didn't understand where they came from. It wasn't until later that I learned from my father that chickens, roosters, horses and cattle were very much a part of the daily scene on an area farm where I had lived and played until my family moved to town and bought a grocery store.

In those days there were no restrictions to keeping a few chickens and roosters in many city neighborhoods.

As a child I couldn't tell you much of the farm where I had lived since birth, but the crowing of a rooster invariably touched a nerve. The clarion call made me unexplainably sad.

To this day the sound of a rooster crowing and the mournful sound of a freight train steam engine cause this older boy to retrace his tracks.

IT TOOK FEWER THAN two dozen well-chosen words to impress on me early in life the obligation and meaning of friendship.

The little drama that had a profound effect occurred at the home of one of my best friends, Carl Fleming. His house had the excitement of a long staircase. The fun was to stick out a foot and brake your slide before you hit that huge round knob at the end of the line. It was a special treat for me since our dwelling didn't have anything as elaborate and that much fun.

More than once Carl's mother had warned us we'd hurt ourselves and get in trouble if we kept sliding down the bannister again and again. This only added to our enjoyment.

And then it happened. On one of the slides Carl's foot hit a lamp at the foot of the steps and the lamp shattered. His mother had gone to the store.

I knew we were in for it, but I couldn't foresee what would happen.

Mrs. Fleming returned home, saw what was left of the lamp and literally hit the ceiling.

"Which one of you boys did this?" she demanded.

There was a loud silence and she repeated her question.

And then knowing from past experience that corporal punishment had been administered to me for offenses far less than this, and possessing a strong sense of survival, I piped up: "Carl did it, but he didn't mean to."

To my childish surprise Mrs. Fleming turned to me, pointed a finger for emphasis and said sternly: "I thought Carl was your friend. A friend doesn't tattle on a friend and get him in trouble."

I don't recall if I said anything else or if or how she punished Carl, but I do recall the impact of that statement. It rang in my ears and mind for days afterwards.

It has served as a beacon and guide in my friendships down through the years.

Mrs. Fleming's words of enlightenment also made me have high expectations of future friendships.

To me a friendship is an oath of trust and loyalty. You do

everything you can to help a friend. You especially do nothing, I repeat, absolutely nothing to hurt him or her.

Sometimes I have been disappointed just as we all have been when we expect too much in return.

Especially since the test of real friendship was driven home to me at the foot of Mrs. Fleming's staircase landing, scattered with glass.

A lamp can be replaced easier than a shattered friendship.

UNCLE SID AND MR. WILKEY are very much a part of my childhood memories.

Uncle Sid helped out in my dad's grocery and Mr. Wilkey had a tiny shoe shop near our store. They were different personalities but there were similarities.

Each was dignified, kind and wise, with a healthy sense of personal identity and pride. But what really impressed this "colorblind" youngster was the fact they listened to what I had to say.

It was rare back then for a grownup to pay much attention to a kid. What could he have to say that was of interest? Yet when I was in the presence of these two esteemed gentlemen I felt my personal esteem zoom upward.

Every now and then when business slacked a little, Uncle Sid listened as I told him about some of the things that happened at school. There were things I would tell him I couldn't tell anyone else, including my own parents.

They might be impatient with me or scold me, but Uncle Sid understood youngsters also have problems that seem heavy to them. He would puff on his old corncob pipe and every now and then shake his head in an understanding way.

On one occasion, I especially recall, I felt my world was closing in on me, and I was thankful Uncle Sid seemed to understand.

We went outside and he let me talk without interruption. When I was talked out Uncle Sid once again gave me this bit of philosophy to think about:

"What will be will be and what ain't to be might accidentally happen. So what's the use of worrying?"

MR. WILKEY WAS a highly respected businessman on Palmetto Street. He had a few shoes for sale in his modest store but he mostly fixed shoes. He was known for his honesty and the quality of his work and some of his customers were white folk from the affluent nearby Vine Street and Oak Street areas.

He also barbered on the side but, as I can personally attest, he was more skilled as a cobbler.

Mr. Wilkey had more spare time than Uncle Sid, and I often had long conversations with him inside his little shop.

I don't remember how well read he was, but I recall he liked to ask deep philosophical questions such as "I wonder why we are here?" and "What is the purpose of life?" And every now and then he seemed to be impressed with an observation I made. "That's interesting," he'd smile with approval. I felt seven feet tall when he said that.

One of the reasons I liked to visit Mr. Wilkey was I appreciated being appreciated and when I was in the confines of that little frame building I felt I was safe from the harshness and criticism of the outside world.

Mr. Wilkey was a kind, gentle man and his approval meant a great deal to a youngster who was hungry for more self-approval and confidence.

There is no doubt in my mind that these and other kind adults played a big role in shaping my behavior and my feelings toward others.

Both of these gentlemen reinforced a belief I've held for

years: One of the finest things you can do for a person, young or older, is to treat that person with kindness, respect and dignity.

.

'I'm Sorry' Can Put Out The Fire

MOST MAJOR BREAKTHROUGHS occur because of insight and because someone is too stubborn to give up.

Conversely, most breakups of marriages and friendships, and rifts that fail to heal, occur because someone is too stubborn to take heed or admit fault.

"I can do it," is an affirmation of confidence in oneself and has been the battle cry of many an artist, businessman, inventor or of an average citizen fighting great odds in order to keep his head above water.

"It's your fault, you did it," is a phrase guaranteed to break down communications and efforts to defuse an argument.

Tenacity, singleness of purpose and sheer stubbornness may help us to achieve our goals and ambitions. Stubbornness, on the other hand, may also be the villain in a rocky marriage, in failing relationships with friends and relatives and in less than top-flight job performance and career success.

A couple of days after a severe windstorm, my wife and I were taking a drive and noticing some mighty looking trees had been literally yanked up by their roots from the force of the gale-like winds. Yet all around these felled giants were much smaller, slender and weaker trees that had survived the fury of the storm.

They had enough flexibility and give to bend to the force of

71

the wind. Not so with the too firmly planted giant trees who refused to give an inch.

HEREIN, I BELIEVE, is a parallel about stubbornness and the use of these magic words: "I'm sorry."

These words have helped prevent or stop many a heated argument at home and at the work place.

So have, "It's my fault" or "It's my mistake."

What is there to continue arguing about when the party of the first or second part accepts the blame for something that has brought on the problem?

We're not advocating that anyone should become a doormat by sacrificing his or her assertiveness and pride. But we've noticed it sometimes takes more strength of character to give in and admit one is wrong than to adamantly refuse to take the blame.

I know of one very smart lady who even goes a step further in the name of harmony and a good marriage. On more than one occasion she has said "I'm sorry" when her husband has fussed and pouted too long over a slight or imagined grievance.

Her husband asked her why she said she was sorry when she wasn't the one at fault. Her reply: "It doesn't matter who's wrong. I'm sorry we had the misunderstanding in the first place. I don't like to see you get upset."

She had already knocked him out by this display of wisdom and tenderness. Then she gave him the double-whammy by telling him, with great emphasis on each little word: "I love you."

"Yeah", he also responded in kind, knowing full well he had lost the silly argument somewhere back down the road when she had stated "I'm sorry" even as he was revving up for another round.

He at least had sense enough to realize his "loss" was their gain.

AN OLD SONG BELTS out the message "You always hurt the one you love," and as with many tunes there is a semblance of truth in the words.

It isn't that you are mean and sadistic and deliberately go out of your way to hurt your partner. But the fact is the closer one feels to another person, the more vulnerable you both are.

A stranger, a passing acquaintance or even a friend won't be as hurt or stung by an ill-considered remark as your own mate. The one you love is in much closer proximity to your interests, your moods, good and bad, and to your overstatements and "misspeak" generalizations. He or she cares about you and what you do and say.

"You always do that" are four words, for instance, that should be banned from the English language were it not for the danger of censorship.

Such outright, flat pronouncements are guaranteed to accelerate any argument by dousing reason and communication with the gasoline of reckless overstatement.

In this age of VCRs, music videos and instant replays, it might be a good idea for some couples to tape and record their spats and then play them again when both sides have cooled off.

Watch and listen closely and see at what point reason and logic take flight and unreasonableness sets in. Does this seem to be worth arguing about and perhaps ruining a meal or an evening or in some cases adding to the strain of an already wobbly marriage?

Do the accusatory exaggerations, strident voices and peeved looks now appear to be more funny than serious?

Also, keep track of the time it took for this domestic storm to blow over and ask yourself just how many minutes and hours even the most long-lived of us have to squander and was it worth the waste and hurt.

THERE IS SOMETHING MORE insidious and dangerous than overheated overgeneralization. It is the failure of some couples to communicate.

This form of "shunning" by one of the partners can have a much more deleterious effect than arguing too heatedly and too much.

"When he gets upset he just clams up," said a wife who by nature is outgoing and likes to communicate with those she is interested in.

"I ask him what is the matter and he just grunts or says nothing is wrong, and I know that we are in for a long period of silence.

"He'll sit there on his recliner with a paper or magazine stuck in his face, and he won't say a word. When I ask him something, he won't answer or he'll reply in one or two words."

The wife says if she tells her stubborn husband that "we need to talk," he'll answer: "You may need to talk. I don't."

She said she has seen him stay in this "kind of a fuming state" for up to a week or more and that during this time she feels like a prisoner, "like a non-person" who doesn't really exist.

She is a very caring person and looks on marriage in the traditional way as a lifelong commitment, but her husband's war of stony silence is taking its toll.

They have been married for many years and "there is now very little communication between us, although there never has been too much.

"I believe," she said, "it would be easier for me to try and live with a mean-talking husband than one who goes into his shell anytime something irritates him.

"This is a kind of abuse you don't hear too much about. It's a form of hell I wouldn't wish on anyone," said this warm, caring person.

Even a recording of this kind of argument wouldn't help. All you'd hear is the deathly silence of a dying marriage, and you'd see a mean, stubborn, brooding person sitting in his recliner with a newspaper up against his nose.

WHEN ONE IS YOUNG and inexperienced it appears to be a sign of weakness to admit to a mistake.

But as you mature and interact with people at home and in the pressure of the work place, it becomes apparent the more secure the individual, the better the chance he or she will take the blame if it is warranted.

As conscientious as he may be, such an individual realizes a goof or error is not the end of the world nor a blanket indictment of his record and worth as a human being. He tries for perfection but doesn't fall to pieces when he misses the mark.

I've noticed that those with the frailest egos are more likely to point the finger of blame away from themselves. A healthy ego can handle the good and the bad, which are the basic ingredients of day-to-day living.

The words "I'm sorry" or "It's my fault" are some of the most important and effective words in the English language.

They can put out those spreading flames. They can also keep arguments from starting.

SO YOU DON'T LIKE
YOUR NAME

I'VE OFTEN WONDERED HOW different my life might have been had my folks named me Biff or Bill or Brad.

Instead, they gave me the unlikely name of Julius.

How often I have wished I was a Jack or a Jim or a Joe. Ed would be fine as would Tom or Bob. Almost anything but Julius or Tyrone or Percy or Bubba would have been all right.

My parents named me after my mother's father, who, I am told, was an unusually "fine, intelligent and handsome" figure of a man.

I never had the privilege of knowing this highly-touted gentleman, but early in life I came to resent him for the name that was imposed on me.

When my schoolwork wasn't up to par, I'd be reminded by my mother that a namesake had the responsibility of living up to high standards. Yeah, and what about the handsome part? How was I going to live up to that part of the grandfather legend? I wasn't scary looking, but I certainly wasn't "star quality."

Tell that to a doting mother of an only child and she'll look at you as if you need double-strength glasses.

Some strange optical illusion takes place when your mother sees you. Her eyes screen and filter out anything that makes you look less than a Hollywood matinee idol. She sees a young man so dazzlingly handsome it almost hurts to look. Where? Where?

As for intelligence, something also happens when your IQ is being evaluated by the least objective person in the world.

"He is like his grandfather. He just needs to settle down and study more."

But then she also thought the name "Julius" had a beautiful ring. That's how objective she was.

WHAT'S IN A NAME? Ask any kid, especially in the early grades of school if he or she enjoys being set apart from his or her peers.

The answer is a definite "no." Anything that makes you seem different from your classmates is "gross."

Included in this category would be un-classy clothes, haircuts and hair styles, unusual tics and shyness or names or faiths that are different.

The name Julius seemed to be a challenge for several of the guys with usual names such as Jack and Jim and John.

So, the ringing of the recess bell was the beginning of another round for a little flyweight named Julius.

I don't know how good my illustrious grandfather was with his fists, but his progeny got plenty of practice. Sometimes I did all right, but other times I paid a price for my handle and came home with a bloody nose and soiled clothes.

One day I got excellent results during a recess "bout." It was one of my better performances, and I was very proud of the way I had dispatched my opponent. He even said he had had enough, the ultimate act of surrender. I described the bout to my father.

Although my father didn't encourage me to get into these schoolyard skirmishes, he was a behind-the-scenes promoter. He kept a low profile because he knew how much my mother abhorred violence and especially its byproduct, dirt.

But he also said if reason didn't work, I should try to take care of myself. "Remember," he said, out of earshot of my mother, "if you ever let a bully chase you home one time, he'll do it from then on."

This was man-to-man talk and I understood what he meant.

So, when this very satisfying "victory" occurred, I could hardly wait to tell my father. Even my mother's scolding would be worth it. Wow, how that dear lady hated dirt and the idea of her son getting hurt, almost in that order it seemed.

My dad smiled the conniving smile of an accomplice as I divulged my triumph.

"And the next time I swung, I hit him right on the chin and that took care of him. Jim didn't want any more."

Actually it was Percy who fell victim, but somehow it seemed the victory wouldn't have been as sweet and important over a kid named Percy. Better it should be over someone with a more formidable name such as Biff or Bill or Brad, or Spike, or Joe.

IT NEVER OCCURRED to me if I so disliked my name I could darn well change it. You don't tamper with your last name very often except for reasons such as Americanizing Polishevsky to Parker a couple of generations ago.

So instead of a first name I didn't like, why not use initials or maybe the Spanish equivalent, Julio? Well, I still wouldn't have a comfortable, everyday name such as Jack.

And I wasn't one of those kids who gets nicknames such as Julie or Bud or Bubba.

But a strange thing happened on the way to adulthood. Somehow my uncommon name started taking on a different meaning. Wasn't I named after "an unusually fine" grandfather I had never known?

And isn't ours a tradition-steeped heritage with a rich history of accomplishments and the ability to survive? A sense of defiance, pride, identity and loyalty began stirring and at some particular point there was no turning back.

Like me and my name and my ancestors or forget it. I wasn't going to fight you on the school grounds anymore, but I was going to stand my ground as to my name and who I am.

Maybe it isn't so bad to be different if you can be proud of it. If it is a proud difference.

MY MOTHER WASN'T the only one who thought Julius was a fine name for a little boy. Her sister also named her son Julius. He was several years younger than the first Julius.

Since he and I were "only" children, we became good friends and playmates.

I was on the wild side and got into much mischief. He was better behaved and got into much less trouble, especially when he wasn't with me.

An example: People usually owned no more than one car back then and one-car wooden garages served their purpose. They were also fun places to climb up. There were all kinds of games you could play. Parachute jumping was coming into vogue, and I wondered how a big umbrella would work if my cousin and I took a jump.

We found out. He got on my back. I stepped off the one-story garage. The umbrella turned inside out. I had the wind knocked out of me. Little Julius was scared but unhurt.

He ran crying to his mother and aunt. Big Julius had done it again.

"You could have hurt little Julius."

Big Julius got spanked when he got his wind back. Little Julius was consoled. That was typical. Whenever they called me it was a loud, emphatic "JULIUS." If they called little Julius it was a lilting, softly musical "J-u-l-i-u-s."

Some people have better luck with names than others.

I WISH I HAD KNOWN at least one of my grandparents from the Old Country.

As it was, I was never privileged to see or know any of them. Fate can be cruel and abrupt in European villages where freedom, human rights, food and the basics of life are scarce commodities.

I wish there had been more of a continuity of generations to trace back and learn from and to cherish. I would have learned a lot about their hardships, sacrifices and disappointments and dreams and the bridge to freedom they provided my parents by being survivors.

I especially wish I'd known you, grandfather. My mother told me you were someone to be proud of. She said you were an unusually fine man and people respected you.

I'm proud of you, Grandpa Julius, for the heritage you gave me.

And thanks for your name. I'm proud of that, too.

It has a nice ring . . . like the freedom I enjoy.

IS THE WORLD
STILL HERE?

MANY MORNINGS WHEN HE walks into the building where he works, he asks the guard at the desk: "Is the world still here?"

And then as he scans the stark headlines that shout about war, threats of war, terrorism and other forms of murder and mayhem, he agrees with the guard's summation: "It's just barely still here."

This has become a daily ritual, a whistling-in-the-dark, half-kidding way of acknowledging the world is in turmoil.

Reading the newspaper accounts and watching television give ample proof of man's inhumanity to man and his inability to peaceably co-exist with his fellow man, and one gets the feeling that peace on earth is an increasingly elusive and unattainable condition.

It makes one wonder if indeed man will manage not only to foul his nest but to blow it to pieces.

Yet, that is only one side of the coin. The fact is that the human race, with all of its contradictions, perversities, selfishness and mean streaks is still here and apparently here to stick around for a long time. That in itself is a miraculous thing, if you stop to think about it.

IN A WAY it is a miracle there aren't more international squabbles, wars and assorted bloodlettings given man's propensity for not being able to get along even on a small scale.

People often find it difficult to lead a peaceful existence in family, office, social or even church settings. So what is the big surprise that they have much more difficulty on a global scale, where distrust and differences in language, customs, ideologies, and cultures fuel the fires of intemperance and misunderstanding?

Basically, if two people who start out being "in love" and who have common interests, including children, find it difficult or impossible to get along, it doesn't augur well for world peace and brotherhood, where hatred and distrust are present before overtures to try and get along are even made.

The next time the newsman asks the guard at about 5 a.m. in the morning: "Is the world still here?" instead of replying:

"It's just barely here," he might answer: "Yes, and it's a miracle, isn't it?"

A Dime Was More Than Ten Cents

I REMEMBER WHEN A DIME was the most popular coin around.

It was during the days when a dime comfortably bought you a good, hot cup of coffee or two and when Five and Dime Stores were basically filled with items for that modest price.

When we say "popular," it doesn't mean we liked having just a dime or dimes in our pocket. All of us would have preferred larger coins, and especially paper money.

But somehow the diminutive dime, which in 1916 was the Mercury dime and since 1946 has borne the likeness of Franklin D. Roosevelt, became a unit of measure in everyday life and in our conversations.

A dime could buy a hamburger and somehow they tasted better than the ones more dimes can now buy. Younger taste buds wouldn't make the difference, would they?

A dime airplane or kite could literally fly you to friendly and exotic skies.

A dime could take up at least 15 minutes of a busy grocery clerk's time as he put together an order of penny candies, each painstakingly and carefully selected by a youthful customer. "No, I'll take the peppermint stick instead." Naturally, it would be at the other end of the candy counter.

A dime could buy a *Saturday Evening Post* and it could buy you a neat toy. And I don't think there was ever a kid who loved toys as much as I did, or one who had so few.

At the time I couldn't understand my parents' close-fisted attitude toward something that was a high priority in my young life.

I hadn't yet arrived at the understanding that the hard times they were going through were compounded by even harder times as youngsters in the Old Country. To them a nickel or dime spent on a toy was a waste of money.

I also didn't realize a lack of toys made me read more and use my imagination more. Reading about pirates and detectives was almost as much fun as playing with a shiny toy. Almost, but not quite.

And if you put your mind and imagination to work, a cardboard or wooden box, especially with wheels, could become an automobile. An old tire could be rolled for many miles without wearing out anything but the roller.

IT'S TIME TO FESS UP. Just how long can a red-blooded active kid get along without at least a small fleet of toy cars?

A nickel or dime saved from lunch or "borrowed" from the cash register would be invested in a toy, not without great guilt and remorse. But the desire to be a "car owner" was more than a small body could stand.

I'd run my hand over my prized possession and feast my eyes on it as I walked toward home. But having this car was a no-no and I didn't want or need the hassle that would follow. So, I'd find a spot which I would remember and hide my treasure in a hurriedly dug out hole.

Maybe they use a better grade of tin and paint these days, but after a day or so, my once shiny car was already rusted. Perhaps it was my first inkling that this is a tinsel and temporary world.

Plastic wrap, where were you when I needed you the most?

Now when I buy my grandchildren toys they don't need or even like, I wonder if an adult is making up for a toy-less childhood. Of course these toys cost much more than a dime and are not nearly as much fun for the buyer or the recipients.

Recently, when I was inspecting a couple of toy cars, a small car aficionado pointed to one of the cars and said: "Mister, that one will go faster than the other one."

I thanked the expert and looked at the shiny red and blue paint which would not be subjected to premature rusting unless carelessly left outside.

More often than not one of the grandchildren will say: "I've got one of those." By now they are into exotic toys which make my little gifts seem very basic.

Yet somehow they still look good to this grandfather whose toys were stealthily purchased by dimes instead of dollars.

NOT WORKING:
A WAY OF LIFE

I AM CONVINCED as important as work is in our lives, most people do not like the jobs they have.

These are not necessarily people who don't like to work. They just don't like what they are presently doing. This is sad and is reflected in the attitude of the worker and the inferior finished product.

Unlike those who refuse to shoulder the responsibility of work, these citizens harness up but get very little enjoyment from their efforts. They literally have to kick themselves in the slats each morning to get going to a job that at best only provides a living and considerable boredom.

Then consider the enthusiasm of those who use work as an outlet for their own expressions. They work with almost loving care and interest and not with the impersonal and unthinking action of a machine.

Unlike those who never do any more than they are paid for — and are usually paid accordingly — the enthusiastic worker will give more than 100 percent of his talents and efforts.

Besides his monetary reward, he gets back an undetermined amount of satisfaction and fulfillment. He is among those who realize happiness is "not in possessions but in the joy of achievement."

Whether he is a professional man, a businessman, a salesman, a secretary, teacher, painter, carpenter, mechanic, doctor or chef, his pride in his work shows through.

There is an extra ingredient that separates him from the run-of-the-mill person just making a living at a job he or she barely tolerates.

A fine, motivated, people-oriented car salesman recently told a customer before the purchase: "You'll enjoy this baby." He lovingly stroked the car's fender as he made the statement.

He sounded as if he meant it. The customer bought the car and learned the salesman was right. Now both are pleased. Enthusiasm is contagious.

HOW GREAT TO FEEL that one has some control in life even if it is in the tiny sphere in which one works.

When we focus in and concentrate on the immediate task at hand, it shuts out much of the world's chaotic clatter and disorder. The world does not seem to be nearly as unwieldy, ominous and unpredictable.

It has seemingly been reduced and compressed to a manageable size, one that can be handled for at least an eight-hour period by the worker who knows and enjoys his task.

In effect, his work not only bolsters his pride, ego, self-reliance and self-identity, it provides him with a safer, more snug haven — one over which he has more control.

Unemployment results in the loss of billions of earned dollars, and potentially valuable manpower goes down the drain. This depletes the gross national product and billions of dollars in taxes go to plug up the vacuum created by unemployment.

The loss of human dignity and pride is inestimable. It is a less tangible loss, but much the greater loss nonetheless.

Work at a job you like, if possible, but at least work at a job.

Of course the truly lucky ones are those who enjoy what they are doing and make work an integral part of their life. Many of these enjoy their work so much they subscribe to the theory that nothing is work unless you'd rather be doing something else.

THOSE WITH WORK ETHICS are sometimes surprised by the lackadaisical and indifferent attitude of the uninitiated who enter the job market.

Their lack of knowledge of even the basic requirements for holding a job is something difficult for the seasoned jobholder to understand.

Would you believe on most jobs it is important to be at work on time? Of course this requires one to go to bed at a reasonable hour in order that he or she may stay awake while at "work."

A chronically late individual after being braced by his boss, stated he never went to bed before 1 o'clock in the morning "because there are some good TV shows I watch every night." His job required him to be to work at 6 a.m. He seldom got there on time.

Others couldn't understand why their superintendents were so testy because they make numerous, long-winded personal calls during office hours. They didn't see the connection between getting paid for 40 hours of work and producing same.

They also didn't understand why it was necessary to call in "sick" so their employer would know they'd be absent. One such worker declared, "They ought to know if I'm not there that I'm sick."

And then there are the sales people and clerks who are not familiar with even rudimentary acts of courtesy.

An acquaintance says he has quit buying gas at a self-service station on Amnicola Highway on his way home because the clerk behind the counter refuses to say "thank you" when he pays for the gasoline.

"The station is convenient, but the clerks are rude," he said. "Not only will they not acknowledge the customer's existence, they even think it's beneath their dignity to crack a smile."

So he drives "four extra miles" to do business "with a pleasant person. I don't have to take discourteous treatment and also pay for it," he said.

Those who have not been taught courtesy or exposed to the work ethic are short-changing the customer and the boss.

Mostly they are cheating themselves.

A Fond Farewell To
'Mr. Wonderful'

Alex Guerry and I literally came from two different worlds.

His forebears arrived on these shores from England in about the year 1635 in search of greater religious freedom. There is no official record of great financial hardships in their genealogy, which can be traced for hundreds of years.

My forebears arrived on these shores from Russia and Poland in search of numerous freedoms denied them in the "Old Country," including religious freedom, the freedom to make a living and almost every other freedom cherished by mankind.

There is no genealogical record of my ancestors that goes beyond their coming to this country in the 1890s. What I know about them was told to me by my mother and father, uncles and aunts.

Even if records had been kept for a while, they would have been lost, burned or otherwise destroyed as generation after generation fled to safer grounds from a Europe not known for its tolerance of those outside of the official religious or political establishment.

Not only did my and Alex's forebears arrive on these blessed shores at different times and from different worlds, they lived in different worlds after they got here.

In plain English, Alex and I traveled in different circles,

financially and socially.

Our backgrounds differed, we didn't belong to the same clubs, we didn't go to the same schools, and Alex, known to his friends as "A," probably never had a bounced check in his life.

SO WHY AM I writing about "A," who died this week from a heart attack?

He doesn't need my stamp of approval for all of the tremendous civic work he did in this city he loved. There are many buildings that are monuments to his tireless drive and vision, including the refurbished Tivoli Theatre and the Soldiers and Sailors Memorial Auditorium.

This town is loaded with examples of his civic pride and interest and they have been listed in other columns and editorials.

The nationally recognized Chattem Inc., which he headed, is a tangible example of his business ability and acumen. He was success-oriented and everything he was interested in became full-bloom under his vital guidance.

The man was a dynamo of energy. I get to work at or before 5 a.m. and many times at this spooky hour, the phone would ring. It was Alex. Sometimes it would be for me. Often as not it would be for John Vass, our business editor.

"A" had something on his mind, and you can bet it usually turned out to be important. "That mind of his never shuts down," John said.

However, this past Wednesday, "A" was stricken while playing tennis and shortly afterward he died.

This town lost one of its biggest boosters and a tremendous mover and shaker who got things done, even if he had to shake someone up. And sometimes that WAS the case.

I MET ALEX at the old YMCA on Georgia Avenue. I was interested in staying in shape and so was "A." I liked handball and so did he, although he was a better handball player than I was and a great racquetball and tennis player.

He was slim and wiry. I was huskier and also lifted weights. But what we shared in common was a spirit of competitiveness. He also went after each point as if it were a point on the stock market. What a competitor!

After games we'd sit around with other "athletes" and have some bull sessions. I loved that old "Y" with its combination of steam, sweat, eucalyptus smells and general informality.

A man could be the head of a billion-dollar firm, but when he took off his street clothes and put on his gym clothes, a lot of facade and sense of importance was also laid aside.

There would be much kidding back and forth. It was usually done in friendly fashion, although sometimes I'd detect a facetious note.

I don't recall ever hearing anyone say this to "A's" face but every now and then you'd hear, "There goes Mr. Wonderful."

I got along great with "A," and I wasn't exactly sure why he earned this title, which clearly indicated he had an exalted opinion of himself.

We had a clique at the "Y" which was named for STUFFED SHIRTS spelled backward. "A" wasn't a member of this raucous group and during one of our noisy restaurant meetings, a member said: "Alex thinks he's something special. He thinks everything he does is the greatest."

MY CURIOSITY CAUSED me to do some research. The guy who befriended me at the old YMCA was not a stuffed shirt. Sure of himself. Sure. He had an ego that was alive and well. But he was not a snob who looked down on someone not in his social or financial circles.

My "research" surprised me. I generally knew something about "A's" achievements. But some of the specifics were:

At Baylor School he had the highest academic average all four of his high school years. He wasn't just an egghead. He was outstanding in a variety of sports.

At the University of the South at Sewanee, he earned Phi Beta Kappa academic honors as a junior and starred in football, basketball and tennis.

He went on to earn a master's degree in business at the University of North Carolina.

Hmmmmm, I thought, this guy really is "something special." He does excel in everything he does.

And then I learned that "A" was a war hero in World War II. I'm talking about a bona fide war hero in the Army Air Corps where he distinguished himself in the South Pacific in a manner that won him numerous high decorations.

I came back home after service in Europe and the Philippines. My highest rank was that of master sergeant. "A" was a highly decorated lieutenant colonel whose exploits were in *Reader's Digest.*

Yet at the "Y" he didn't pull any rank on me. We respected each other as competitive athletes and probably as near-workaholics.

So what was with the "Mr. Wonderful" description? "Alex thinks he's something special," said the fellow in our little social club. "He thinks everything he does is the greatest."

My research turns out he was "something special" and everything he tackled turned out to be "the greatest" whether it was in school, in combat, for which he volunteered, or in the rough and tough business world.

"A" knew only one speed — full speed ahead — whether he was flying in combat, guiding Chattem to national prominence or spearheading a civic endeavor.

Could there have been a tinge of envy or outright jealousy from a lesser light for an original, a unique achiever who was never satisfied with second place?

He was born with great advantages, but he didn't let that stifle his ambition and drive. Had he been born in a log cabin he would have put siding on it.

His children inherited this "be a winner" attitude.

HERE IS SOMETHING else about "Mr. Wonderful." He not only took his duties and civic projects seriously, he also was concerned with children and adults who needed financial and other help. This he would give in the best biblical sense. He did it quietly and without fanfare.

There is no way of knowing the full extent of "A's" charitable contributions. He had a bigger heart than some realized.

He also loved Chattanooga dearly as demonstrated by his annual Dorothy Patten "Love of Chattanooga Award" given for outstanding service and love of this community. Dorothy Patten, a family member, was an outstanding Broadway actress.

"A" was a highly focused individual and a fierce competitor. He was a fighter and a war hero. His fighting instinct served him well in civilian life and helped save his life during the seventies.

During that time "A" was running on a track in Houston when he suffered a cardiac arrest and collapsed. Luckily, he received CPR from a physician who was nearby and then paramedics arrived with a Lown Defibrillator, a device invented by Dr. Bernard Lown to be used in getting heart beats back to normal. "A's" heart was at a near standstill for two minutes. On the third try his heart got going again.

Dr. Lown, the internationally known Boston cardiologist, co-founded a group that received the 1985 Nobel Peace Prize. He is professor emeritus at the Harvard School of Public Health.

Alex became a close friend of Dr. Lown and credited him with saving his life. In 1987 Alex was elected to the Boston-based board of trustees of the Lown Cardiovascular Research Foundation.

LAST YEAR at about this time, my old ticker started acting up a little. I was occasionally having some irregular beats. That and a few other problems caused me to see a terrific doctor in town. His expertise and prescriptions helped greatly.

But "A" heard from another colleague that I was having ticker problems. He usually came up to my desk at the newspaper and casually mentioned I should lose weight and get back to my "Y" shape, which he maintained. Sometimes for emphasis he'd pat me on my belly and smile that million-watt smile of his.

But this time he said, "I hear you're having some problems. Let me call my secretary and get the company plane ready for you, and we'll fly you to Boston. I'll call Dr. Lown and make an appointment for you."

"When?" I asked kiddingly.

"How about tomorrow?" said Mr. Get-it-done.

How about that, indeed. Is that an old "Y" friend or not?

I didn't take "A" up on his offer, and it was hard for him to understand my reasoning. I'm one of those characters who tries to minimize physical problems.

This may not be smart, but that's the way it is. Besides, I already have a fine doctor.

I thanked him from the bottom of my heart and hope he understood my gratitude for his concern and friendship. I even had our mutual friend, Roy Exum, explain my squeamishness at all things medical.

SO LONG "Mr. Wonderful." You WERE "something special."
And just about everything you did WAS "the greatest."

You were an original. There will never be anyone quite like
you.

We came from different worlds, but there was tolerance.

We lived in different worlds, but there was mutual respect.

TIME AND MACHINES
WAIT FOR NO MAN

IT CAME ABOUT because Betty and I, along with many people in the civilized world, have become increasingly conscious of the role exercise plays in our physical well-being.

In a small room that we refer to as our gym, we have a stationary bicycle, a few weights left over from more active days and a cable exerciser which seems to gain more resistance each year.

Of course there is the walking that can be done around Central High School during the week. The hills and steps and the school's track bring out numerous health-conscious citizens, especially on Sunday.

However, there are those who don't like to walk in hot weather or too cold weather or when it is sprinkling.

My wife convinced me a treadmill would be a good thing to have since she doesn't particularly like to walk outdoors. I bought the idea, literally and figuratively.

But before I worked up enough energy to buy this piece of equipment, my wife had become fascinated with a commercial that showed a young person having a great time as she skied on a simple looking contraption.

"Look at the exercise she's getting by doing that," said Betty.

"Those things aren't too expensive. I think it would be nice to get one."

Betty seemed so excited about skiing in place and getting a good workout that I went along with her. The girl in the commercial did seem like she was having a great time as well as getting a vigorous workout.

SO WE WENT to the sports equipment store and took a look. Our little "gym" would be able to accommodate the ski machine and the treadmill.

It was fun to contemplate using this stuff, and it was satisfying to think this would help tone our muscles and lower our blood pressure.

More importantly, if it helped us stick around for a long time and to enjoy each other and a better quality of life then it was worth its weight in gold.

I have an athletic background which began with my boyhood use of the old YMCA and its equipment, which included a rowing machine.

Eureka! This was like old home days. I felt a rejuvenating surge of energy as I gazed at the shiny rowing machine. It took me back to the old "Y" and the way a young man vigorously pulled the oars on a mostly wooden machine.

The sleek, modern rowing machine bore little resemblance to the rugged but simple machine at the "Y," but it was a rowing machine. It also was reasonably priced and would fit neatly into our little gym.

"It's easy to put together," the young salesman said.

He didn't realize he was talking to one of the most unmechanical people in the world. I'm well coordinated, but mechanics is not my strong point.

The salesman said not to worry. For a few more dollars the ski machine and the rower could be assembled and delivered to our house, along with the treadmill.

The athletic young man also showed us how well the ski machine, the treadmill and the rower worked. It was fun watching him, especially as he gracefully skied.

"You'll love it," he said. We told him we were looking forward to it.

I HAVE LONG believed everyone should have something to look forward to. It adds a joy and dimension to living, not to mention a sense of excitement.

Betty and I could hardly wait for the athletic equipment to be brought to our house. We told them to deliver it after 1 o'clock.

No company delivers anything on time. It usually arrives when the doorbell rings at dinner time. On this day, however, I got home 15 minutes past 1 o'clock, and there was a note on the door saying there was no one home. It was disappointing but only heightened my sense of excitement for the next delivery a few days off.

The exercise sets were finally delivered and arranged in our little gym and naturally placed so we could watch television while exercising. This is the modern way of making exercise more palatable. Some of us don't believe there is no gain without pain.

We could hardly wait to start exercising. Usually one of us rides the bike and then the other comes downstairs. But this time we were an exercise team.

Betty tried out the treadmill and gradually increased the speed. She was delighted with the result. "Now I can walk anytime I feel like it, rain or shine or cold or hot."

I go in more for the old concept of walking on a surface that doesn't move, but I had to admit it was fun changing the speed on the machine-geared walker, which is plugged into an electrical socket.

It also has a panel which shows heart and pulse rate as well as miles and speed. The pulse rate is taken with a gadget one attaches to the ear lobe. This was too clinical for us. The rest of it is fine.

"NOW LET'S TRY the ski machine," said my wife.

She had visions of the pretty little thing on the TV commercial doing her thing as she used her legs and ski poles in perfect rhythm. The young salesman also made skiing seem fun.

Betty did fine until she walked up to the machine and put a foot into the stirrups. There was nothing solid to hold on to but the pole, which also moved.

By the time I helped her get her foot into the other stirrup shoe, I knew we were in trouble.

"Hold me, I'm about to fall," my wife pleaded. "There isn't a thing easy about this," she said as she swayed unsteadily. "Please help me get off before I break my neck."

I hadn't turned her loose the whole time and I wasn't about to. Not only had she not gotten into the ski mode, but she found it tough to just stand there. The ski boots seemed to have a mind of their own as they wiggled back and forth.

I finally extricated her from the "killer" ski machine, and she breathed a sigh of relief. "And they made it look so easy," she gasped. "I'll never try that again."

I'm more athletically inclined than Betty, so I told her I'd show her how it works and that she'd eventually get the hang of it.

I too almost broke my neck. For the record, my wife and I are not skiers and never will be.

BY THIS TIME my wife wasn't about to try the rowing machine. The ski machine had intimidated her.

But I wanted to try it. I'd forgotten how difficult it is to sit down on an object just a few inches off the ground. I finally managed, and Betty helped me get my feet in the stirrups.

Felt like old times pulling back and rowing forward. Like old YMCA days.

But I realized how times had changed when I tried to stand up. I couldn't. Luckily Betty was there to help me.

When she retreated upstairs I thought: " This is ridiculous. I can do this by myself."

I managed, with great effort, to get into position for rowing. And then it was time to get up.

Now for the highlight of the exercising machine experience: I tried to stand up. Uh, oh, I couldn't. The only thing to do was to roll over on my side and then on to my stomach like a beached whale. I finally got to my knees. Luckily, there was a stool nearby, and I grabbed a rung and slowly managed to pull myself upright.

What a humbling experience for an athlete of yesteryear.

No, we aren't going to send back the ski machine and the rowing machine. The kids and grandkids will probably use them without any trouble at all.

It's not the machines' fault. Their parts are much newer and just work a lot better than ours.

A 'Hungry Tiger'
Can Help You Run

Why does a job mean more to one person than to another?

The simplistic answer would be: "Because he or she needs it more." And in many instances this may be true. Yet there is an underlying factor which makes the biggest difference.

Call it attitude, pride, or a stronger work ethic, the fact remains there are those who tackle a job — almost any job — with the determination to not only get it done, but to do it right.

There are also those who consider work — almost any work — to be a burden which eats into their leisure hours and therefore should be muddled through with the least expenditure of energy.

One factor is conditioning. Most who lived during the era of the Great Depression will never again have a cavalier attitude toward work. Obtaining any kind of a job during extremely lean years was a major accomplishment.

Even a youngster recalls the starkness of those days and that when the head of a household proudly announced: "I've got a job," no one even asked what the job consisted of. It didn't matter. What did matter is there would now be some income where before there had been none.

Awareness of hard times has also not been lost on most

immigrants who come to this country. Some citizens complain these newcomers "snatch up any kind of a job" to the detriment of native-born Americans, who are more selective and frown at the low wages involved. Many of our native-born citizens claim they are better off on welfare and therefore opt to stay in a cycle that in some instances has involved two and three generations.

A CAMBODIAN COOK in one of the more popular Chinese restaurants is not only knowledgeable about food and spices, he has the gifted imagination of a master chef. Yet, his formal schooling was pointed toward architecture and engineering.

Someday he hopes to finish his schooling and put his higher learning to practical use, but as of now he is "proud to make a living as a cook." When you've been through unbelievable hardship and deprivation, you don't look down your nose at any job.

"I would someday like to have the opportunity of being an architect, but I would be ungrateful if I didn't appreciate the job I now have," he said. "My employers are very fair and considerate, and I am able to provide for my family (a wife and two small children) and that is now uppermost in my mind."

Does he understand the lack of enthusiasm some people have for their jobs, jobs they say are beneath them or don't suit them and are unfulfilling?

He said he understands but it doesn't alter the fact "we are coming from different directions.

"When you have nothing, you doubly appreciate having something, although that may not seem like very much to someone else. It is all relative."

He added, "But when you get used to being given something, that takes away some of the drive to succeed. There is an old saying that no one runs as fast as when he is being chased by a hungry tiger."

Hunger and poverty have motivated many people. Others have been caught and devoured.

THE EXTERMINATING company had been told on numerous occasions by Betty that Friday is a good day for the technician to come by. Friday is the day the housekeeper is at the home in addition to Betty, who might be at the store or elsewhere at the time.

On numerous occasions the technician would show up on the wrong day.

This past week a company veteran rang the doorbell, not on the designated day, and apologized for the young man who didn't show up as requested. "Good help is hard to get," he said, as he got his foot in the door and proceeded to spray the premises.

He is an interesting character and after a few moments we were discussing work attitudes.

"I've seen 'em come and go," he said, "and the first day I take one of them out on the route I can usually tell whether he's going to make it.

"For instance, this young fellow went with me the first day and after we'd been on the route for about an hour he asked me if we could stop and get some coffee. I told him there was nothing wrong in getting a cup of coffee and we stopped and had a cup. He wanted another one, but I told him we had to move along."

In another hour or so the young man asked: "Is there a store around here that's got a pinball machine? I'd like to play one a little while."

This time the veteran termite technician said, "No, we're not going to do that."

"In about another hour he asked me what time we knocked

off for lunch, and a couple of hours later he wanted to know when did we quit for the day."

The veteran said, "It wasn't any problem figuring out he wasn't going to make it through his probation. You know what he asked me just before I let him off for the day? He wanted to know how much vacation time the company gave and what other benefits we had. That was all he was interested in.

"Nawww," he replied to a question. "We didn't hire him. Out of all of those questions he asked, he didn't ask one about getting rid of bugs and termites."

THE CAMBODIAN immigrant's philosophy about work is not so different from millions of immigrants who came to these shores numerous decades ago.

They viewed America as the land of opportunity, not for a free ride, but for the opportunity of obtaining a job to make a living for their family.

This from a proud naturalized citizen:

"Freedom means many things, including the right to try and even fail. In the Old Country, you didn't have that kind of freedom. If your father was a ditch digger or a blacksmith, so were you. You never had the chance to rise above your station in life. Everything was cut and dried.

"People in this country take too many of their freedoms for granted, including the freedom to work at whatever job they can get."

The cook, with an eye toward his future as an architect, said he sees dignity in any kind of honest work.

"Before I became a cook," he said, "I was a busboy. If I had looked with contempt on my work I would either still be a busboy or out of work."

He added, "Maybe I have not been Americanized enough to understand, but to me there is more dignity in doing any kind of honest work than in depending on help from the government."

I have the feeling he will never become that "Americanized."

HE MUST HAVE DONE
SOMETHING RIGHT

A FRIEND HAS BEEN married 40 years and he considers himself "a very lucky man."

He describes his wife as "a jewel of a lady," who sometimes understands him better than he understands himself.

"She has put up with a bunch of nonsense from me. In looking back I'm eternally grateful. I'd be lost without her," he said.

We asked him to share some pointers with those who want a lifetime marriage.

"I'm a heck of a guy to give advice," he said. "I've made practically every mistake in the book, but maybe that's what qualifies me. I think I've learned from those mistakes."

He added, "I'll tell you one mistake I haven't made and that is not letting my wife know that I love her. That's probably the big reason why she was able to stay with me, especially during those difficult early years.

"I can't understand married people who never tell each other how they feel and seldom show their emotions except to argue. I suppose that's why they print so many anniversary cards that say 'I know I don't tell you I love you during the year, but you know I do.'

"My wife and I never buy that kind of a card. I don't think a day goes by without assurances of how we feel about each other."

Warming to the task of being an expert, he added: "This sounds corny, but I do believe love conquers all. I think if there is enough love and care between two people they can overcome all kinds of obstacles.

"Our marriage is a prime example of that," he said. "We come from different backgrounds, we were raised in different parts of the country and we have different interests."

He said their tastes differ widely in the books they read and in the television programs they like, although there are several shows they enjoy watching together.

"I like sports and enjoy participating in various physical activities and exercises. My wife would just as soon not perspire or have her hair get out of place.

"Sports hold no interest for her. But after all of these years she's still very interested in this old boy.

"If that sounds like I'm bragging, so be it.

"And that's the way I feel about her."

ACCORDING TO the "expert," the differences in tastes and hobbies aren't crucial in a marriage and neither are differences of opinions about politics and other things.

"What matters is if there is agreement on priorities and what is important in your lives, in your personal relationship."

He said the reason some marriages don't last "is simply because two people don't like each other enough to allow not only for differences but even for peculiarities and idiosyncrasies.

"No matter how close you may be and how much you love each other, you've got to be willing to overlook certain things and to allow the other person some space. You may be a married couple, but you are still two separate individuals with separate needs and thoughts. Sometimes you've got to give when you don't feel like it."

The husband said too many married people are so busy running around "trying to have a good time" they don't have enough time to get acquainted with each other, or even the children.

"How are you going to be willing to spend a lifetime with someone if that someone remains a stranger to you?

"Besides," he said, "I know many married people for whom being together for hours at a time is like being sentenced to cruel and unusual punishment.

"You know you're on the right track when you start looking forward to being together and not necessarily on vacation, but at home where you can enjoy each other's company.

"When you get to that point," he said, "you know you are doing something right and you are reaping the greatest rewards of marriage: friendship and togetherness...the opposite of loneliness, one of the things most of us fear the most."

HE CONSIDERS IT elementary to mention that consideration and respect are two highly important ingredients of marriage.

He asked, "How can you stay married to a person who doesn't respect you or one whom you don't respect? And of course there has to be trust."

He added, "Not one of us is perfect and always does the right thing or the thing that always pleases the other. But even when we make a mistake on occasion, we can pick up the pieces and try again.

"Just because someone breaks a dish while washing the dishes doesn't mean that person can never again be trusted to wash dishes, if you get my drift."

The 40-year-married "lucky guy" said he couldn't stress enough that differences don't make that much of a difference in a successful marriage as long as the marriage is built on love and caring.

"I don't have to think for a second to know that my wife is the best friend I have in the whole world. Who else is going to care about me and worry about me the way she does if anything goes wrong? She also believes in the 'for better or worse' part of the marriage vows, something many people forget after they marry.

"And who else will share my joys and victories the way she does? That's what I mean when I say I don't know what I'd do without her. I hope to God I never find out. That's how much I love that little woman."

He said he has taken great pride over the years to see her grow into a much more secure and self-reliant individual who is able to get things done "in her corner of the world."

The husband said his wife began working years ago when "the birds flew out of the nest" and as a result she has more interests which she can share with him.

"We often talk about the kind of day we had at the office and reassure ourselves that those we work for are very lucky to have such reliable and brilliant people to depend on."

Most importantly, he said, is the "wonderful institution" of marriage, in which two people can share their lives and lean on each other for support and comfort "and not be lonesome."

LET'S ALSO HEAR it for a good sense of humor in contributing to marital longevity. He believes some of the "little girl and little boy" should always remain in the wife and husband respectively. "It's more fun that way."

He said, "My wife dislikes football as well as most other sports, and during the Super Bowl game I was practically banished downstairs to watch TV in the playroom. Besides, I wanted her to see the program she liked.

"While I sat there alone, eating nuts from a small bowl, I wished she were a sports fan and could be watching the game with me. It would be more exciting."

During the half his wife urged him to "come upstairs" and sit with her until the game resumed.

And then there was a glimmer of hope for the husband. His wife said she wanted to ask him a question about football.

"Maybe she's getting interested," he thought.

The question: "Honey, who decides who sings the National Anthem before the game starts?"

"Who cares?" the husband laughed with affection.

"I do," replied his wife. "I'm curious about that. Haven't you ever wondered?

"No, I haven't," said the husband giving her a big hug and wondering what he'd ever do without her.

WHEN 'CHARACTERS' WERE MORE COLORFUL

THERE ARE AND HAVE always been "characters." Some are lovable, some lovable and outlandish and others just outlandish.

But the characters of yesteryear seem to be more unique than those of the present day, and I have a theory for this.

Nowadays most people of some note have arrived at their present status or position through a mass education system that trims off their rough edges in cookie cutter fashion. Most of them have at least a high school education, and many have gone to college.

Many characters of several decades ago, however, came up in an era where street smarts and the instinct for survival determined the success of their careers even more than a formal education.

Some were not educated; others were. All were sharp and had more than their share of common sense.

For instance, I can't think of my old courthouse beat without a great deal of fondness for many in that grand old building. Henry Grady comes to mind.

He was a handsome, wavy-haired young assistant attorney general in the office of Atty. Gen. W. Corry Smith. Henry took politics seriously, especially when he actively disliked the incumbent, in this instance a sheriff.

So when he heard that Fred Rutledge was running against the incumbent, he rubbed his chin in his characteristic way and decided he would help Rutledge with his speeches.

HE WAS GOOD with words and Rutledge had some rip-roaring speeches which took pot shots at the incumbent sheriff.

This was before television was the most popular game in town, and hundreds turned out for candidates' meetings because they were fun, free and exciting.

Henry wrote speech after fire-eating speech for Rutledge, who got pretty good at giving them. He was running against a popular sheriff, and he knew his work was cut out for him.

Rutledge told Henry on numerous occasions he appreciated his help. He considered the assistant attorney general as sort of a manager in an undeclared kind of way.

Henry promised him he would help right up to the time he was elected.

Came election day and Rutledge asked Henry to accelerate his efforts for him. "Sure will," said Henry, who resided on Lookout Mountain.

That night the vote was counted, and Rutledge didn't receive a single vote in Henry Grady's precinct. Rutledge saw Henry at the courthouse the next morning and made a beeline for him. He was full of righteous indignation and minced no words as he pointed out Henry hadn't even voted for him.

"Wait just a minute," said Henry, who was always good with words. "This is supposed to be a secret ballot. How in the devil did I know NOBODY on the mountain was going to vote for you?"

Rutledge told me afterwards he was disappointed at losing the election and Henry's "friendship."

CONSTABLE CANDIDATES ran for the not-so-heralded office which then existed in Hamilton County. Those not in the know wondered why anyone would even run for this lowly office.

Jake Jones was among the candidates and was probably the burliest and most outspoken of the lot.

I was having a bite at the beanery across from the paper at the time and Jake, who was not a man to mess around with, asked me in that gruff tone of his:

"Parker, you write stories about these other candidates in the race. How come you don't write something about me running for constable?"

I looked at Jones and at my companions at the table and said what I thought would get me off the hook:

"Well, when you come up with a statement giving a good reason why you're running for constable, I'll write something about you."

Jones, not to be denied, thought a couple of seconds and said:

"Write down that I'm running for constable due to world conditions."

I know a story when I hear or see one, and I did write it down. In fact it made page one as a "bright" and then was carried around the country by the Associated Press.

It got such a reaction that Constable Jones put a sign on his car stating why he was making the race — "Due to world conditions."

ANOTHER SHERIFF candidate wasn't getting too much response at the candidate rallies.

He was not a very prepossessing person at a time when a sheriff was supposed to look like a sheriff in a sort of John Wayne fashion.

Most of the time after one of his so-called speeches, he would wind up with only a couple of applauding spectators, and they didn't sound very enthusiastic. And when his wife and mother finally stopped coming to the meetings, Charlie lost what little audience support he had.

It didn't take him long to realize there was something lacking either in his delivery or the content of his remarks.

He asked me what I thought, and I tried to be kind by suggesting that if he pulled out of the race, it would be less damaging to his ego. But Charlie was determined to "fight on."

Oh well, it was HIS ego that would take a beating, until one night, Eureka! Charlie had inadvertently made a statement that caught the crowd's attention.

He said, "If you folks elect me to be your sheriff, you will NEVER LIVE TO REGRET IT."

There was a slight pause before the audience got the full impact of this remark and then it was bedlam. The audience literally broke up in laughter and mock-supportive cheers.

The sheriff candidate beamed as he warmed himself in his first big audience response.

"Say it again, Charlie," shouted some wag who probably enjoyed dissecting frogs in and out of the laboratory. And he did say it again and again at this and every other election meeting.

Talk about name recognition, Charlie finally got it. Very few votes, but most people in the county heard about the sheriff candidate and his inadvertent but amusing threats to the public welfare.

AND THEN THERE WAS the judge who took note there were numerous prominent people in court who "took the time to be here in your behalf."

The case had to do with a gardener hitting another gardener with a fence post and almost doing him in.

The judge said, "I'm going to take into consideration that this is your first time in court and that the victim has fully recovered. Also, the fact that so many prominent people are here in your behalf tells me something about you.

"But," he admonished, "you can't go around hitting people on the head with fence posts and think you can get by with it. If you're ever here in court again, I'll throw the book at you."

"Judge, your honor," the defendant replied, "it wasn't my idea to be here in the first place."

The judge, known for his laid back informality, joined in the courtroom laughter before finally sounding the gavel.

THOSE WERE THE DAYS for characters in and out of court and in and out of politics.

I had just returned from covering national political conventions when I came down to earth at a jam-packed town hall meeting.

It was during the heat of summer and the low-ceilinged room was free of air-conditioning. Many in the audience fanned themselves as they waited for the serious matters ahead.

With deference to the stifling heat, one of the commissioners suggested that a synopsis of the minutes be given so the meeting could proceed.

So it was. The shorter version was read, but then someone in the room shouted: "That's not all the minutes. Why don't they read all the minutes?"

"I'll tell you why," said a rather large woman who stood up. All eyes were riveted on her, waiting for her answer. "Because they're all a bunch of crooks, and they don't want you to hear all the minutes. That's why."

The audience laughed and so did the maligned officials. It was too hot to argue about her opinion of them. And the meeting proceeded to more important town hall business.

THE MOST BEAUTIFUL FACE
I EVER SAW

I FIRST HEARD ABOUT the Statue of Liberty and Ellis Island from my parents.

They described the ordeal of storm-tossed ocean trips with less than first-class accommodations. In fact, "accommodations" was euphemistic for unbelievably crowded and dangerous conditions aboard ship in a journey which took weeks, not days.

Back then first class wasn't all that great. But second and third class had no class at all.

Yet there was class in the hearts and minds of these people. They didn't expect the government to go out of its way in giving them guarantees. They already had the best guarantee they had ever obtained: The guarantee of freedom and opportunity.

Each time I think of a 14-year-old, making his ocean voyage alone to a land in which he knew no one, I almost burst with pride. That was my father who did that, and he paved the way for freedom for generations to follow. He had never been away from his little town in Poland and here he was an ocean traveler.

When he arrived in America, there was Lady Freedom to greet him. She was standing there with her torch of welcome and that noble expression on her face.

She was the only one to greet him. He was a stranger in a new land. But her greeting was enough to reassure this man-child that he had made the right decision, that everything would be all right.

His mother had placed a few meager dollars in a small pouch which he kept underneath his shirt, fastened to a narrow chain around his neck.

He told me he must have touched that pouch a thousand times before he finally got off the ship. The pitifully few dollars would have to last him until he got a job. There were no relatives or friends to help him. There were also no welfare checks or food stamps.

"I didn't speak the language," he told me. "But I knew a very important word."

The word was 'work,' and he immediately put it to maximum use.

ONE OF HIS FIRST JOBS was shoveling snow around the clock on the streets and sidewalks of New York. Another one of his earlier jobs was in a place full of steam, but I can't recall that particular line of work.

I do remember he said the steam vapors and heat sometimes caused some of the adult workers to faint. "I never fainted," he proudly told me. "I had to prove I was a man although I was still a boy."

He said he stuck with this for several months until he found a job as a painter.

Had he ever painted before? No, but he was a quick learner and soon became a boss painter for an apartment owner by the name of Harrison.

By the time he got to the top floor apartments "it was time to start all over again on the bottom floor."

Mr. Harrison treated him as his son and he became a favorite in the family, living and eating with them.

But a few years into his painting career he told a surprised and disappointed Mr. Harrison he was moving to Chattanooga to go into farming. One of his friends had moved here and wrote glowing reports about the beautiful countryside. My father had a great love of land and nature. He also had a burning desire to be his own boss.

He told me he made up his mind when he saw how a previously praised painter fell in the esteem of tenants.

"They used to say, 'when you have my apartment painted, be sure and send Sol to do the job. He's the best.' But in a few years they were saying 'don't send old Sol, send anybody else. Sol is blind as a bat. He can't see what he's doing."

Sol wasn't losing his eyesight, my father said. They just didn't like his work anymore. He said he took a lesson from Sol and bought a farm in the Silverdale area. My mother intensely disliked country life, and the farmhouse and barns later caught on fire. I don't believe there was a connection. There also was no insurance.

His next venture was the grocery business in Chattanooga, a successful move in which my mother worked side by side with him. I was also pressed into service at an early age.

The key word here was also "work." They didn't expect anyone to give them anything else. Had they not already been given one of the greatest gifts on earth, freedom? This included the freedom to work at whatever they chose. And work they did.

They also expected their son to work at the store and at school. To have an opportunity for a good basic education and not take advantage of such a privilege; that would have been "a sin."

There was always the spoken and unspoken goal to better oneself.

FROM MY PARENTS, I learned that one group of people who appreciated this country are those who came here from "over there."

And from my military experience, I learned the other group which genuinely appreciated the United States consists of veterans who have been "over there" and who were lucky enough to come back here.

Tears of joy welled up in my eyes when I returned from wartime Germany and saw the Statue of Liberty welcoming me home.

She was not just an impressive statue. In a sense she was as alive and real as if she were flesh and blood.

Young men had risked their lives for her. Some had paid the ultimate price. Others would be crippled for life.

The lady appreciated the effort in behalf of the freedom which she exemplified. Her protective expression was reassuring to those of us who were returning from the hell of war.

There was also a wistful sadness for those who didn't return.

Our Liberty Ship steamed into shore as Lady Liberty welcomed us. My God — she was beautiful!

At that precise moment I had never felt closer to my brave, immigrant parents.

It's Not Easy To Forgive Yourself

PARENTS, PERHAPS MORE THAN OTHERS, fall into the trap of putting excessive blame on themselves.

Recently, a parent confided: "I've almost come to the conclusion my husband and I have made some terrible mistakes in raising our kids that have caused them to have problems in their married life.

"I know these are different times," she said, "but when three of your four children have been divorced twice, you begin asking yourself, 'Where have we gone wrong?'"

She said she and her husband have often asked this question and, search as they may for an answer, the answer eludes them. "Especially since we've been married all of these years and have never given our children the feeling our marriage was not going to be permanent."

Some divorced people blame broken homes and unhappy home lives during their nurturing years, "but whom can our children blame for their marital problems?"

She said if she and her husband had an occasional disagreement, "the way all married people do," they would try to resolve it in private and not let the children "in on it."

Seeing the marriages of their children dissolve, one after the other, has been "one of the low points of our lives," she said.

121

"The court proceedings and divorces have been heart-breaking and hard to take. And to make matters worse, there are seven grandchildren involved and the divorces have considerably changed our relationships with them.

"We don't get to see them nearly so often as we once did, and it hurts us more than anyone can realize who hasn't gone through this sort of trauma."

The lady had enough on her mind without my pointing out what some psychologists and marriage counselors claim, that wives and husbands who keep too low a profile in regard to disputes give their children an unrealistic expectation of what married life should be.

Since mom and dad "never argued" — the heck they didn't — we (their children) must not be getting along too well because we argue most of the time and our marriage must be failing.

That's one theory, and there are thousands of others, some which seem to make sense and others which only add to the complexity of trying to figure out what is right and wrong. Meanwhile, conscientious parents will always wonder where they went wrong even if they apparently did almost everything right.

"Our children can't say we didn't give them every opportunity we knew of to help them grow into happy, stable, intelligent adults who could keep a marriage together," she said.

"Back in those days I felt like I was driving a taxi cab. I was forever taking them to scout meetings, to school, to dancing school, to music school, to the YMCA and to many other places.

"It never occurred to me to feel I was being used, that I was putting my own feelings and wishes on hold. My husband and I worked hard, but we felt it would pay off in many ways and that our children would benefit by our advice and examples.

"But it didn't turn out that way, and now we wonder just where we did go wrong."

She said it was ironic because there are some families where hardly a kind word is spoken between husband and wife, much less affection shown, and that in these families many of the children marry "and stay married just the same way we have."

And because the couple can't explain this in a logical fashion there is a tendency to blame themselves. "It just doesn't make sense," she said.

Neither does walking around with a king-sized guilt complex after you feel you have done your part.

FORGIVING YOURSELF is important for good emotional health.

Sure we've all made mistakes. But you didn't go out of your way to hurt someone, did you? Even wives and husbands who love each other are not mistake-free.

Maybe you are an "old school" parent who learned to be overly strict with your children from "older school" parents. In retrospect, you feel you should have spent more time enjoying them and explaining things to them and less time being the strict parent.

There is a tendency to blame oneself for lack of patience and understanding. But to what avail?

Hopefully, children will learn to love and respect their parents more each year the way we have learned to do. And hopefully they will forgive their parents just as we have forgiven ours. They also didn't do everything right even though they tried.

But the big effort is to forgive yourself for the well-meaning mistakes you made.

Those you forgive aren't perfect and neither are you.

Ex-Fighter Pilot Helps Them 'Land' on Feet

IT WAS ONE OF THE MOST inspirational evenings I have ever spent.

I had an idea the occasion would be full of excitement, drama and a little edginess, but I never could have guessed its full impact.

When it was over, I felt uplifted, supercharged, re-energized, awed and thrilled with the determination and basic courage of valiant members of the human race. It was that kind of an event, the 197th class graduation of the local Dale Carnegie course.

Our main interest in attending was a son who was a member of the class. His brother was an alumnus of some years ago, who had recommended the course.

But Betty and I found ourselves caught up in some 30 success stories as each of the graduates introduced guests and gave short talks. Later in the program they made longer talks prior to being presented graduation certificates.

I've done my share of listening to luncheon, after-dinner and political speeches, some made at national conventions and other important forums. But none of these speeches was as riveting, as heart-warming, as genuine as the talks made by these "grads." Some were more personal and revealing than others, but all had the ring of truth.

The talks were timed and the introductions and acknowledgements were short, but the hours slipped by because there were many presentations. So what? There is nothing boring about watching poignant success stories unfold and seeing and hearing the pride manifested all around the banquet room.

IT WAS EASY TO PICK out the proudest person at the graduation. He was the one who gestured and smiled and nodded his head with appreciation and approval and gave praise and encouragement at every turn.

And there were many such opportunities as speaker after speaker made his or her point or got an appreciative chuckle from the audience.

The proud catalyst is Mike Wilson, the instructor of the Dale Carnegie course. He is also thought of as the cheerleader and the guru, who exerts a near-mystical influence on the group.

"I'm proud of you," he'd tell this or that speaker. "A fine job. I knew you could do it," and "that was great."

The praise drew heart-felt "thanks" from the speakers. One of them told me, "I'm not a youngster, but this is one of the proudest moments of my life. I'll be eternally grateful to that man right there."

I found myself watching this gem of a motivator almost as much as the speakers. His enthusiasm is contagious. Naturally, he is a fine speaker, and in a succinctly clear way he summed up the positive points of each speaker and speech.

His wife, Jane, is also involved with him in this business of motivating people and helping them reach toward their "full potential." His job is to stress the positive and to minimize the negative aspects of life, including the habit of useless worry.

He urges a positive approach to life in general, not just in speechmaking.

"I'LL TELL YOU how positive and forceful he is," said a member of the class.

"I had finally signed up but I didn't think I could go through with it. All I could see in front of me was 14 weeks of sheer terror. I hated to get up in front of a group and make a talk.

"I thought about it over the weekend and then I went to see Mike on Monday, the day of the first day of class. I told him I had decided to back out.

"He asked me what the chief reason was. Why I wanted to quit before I even started."

He said, "I leveled with him. I said, 'fear and terror.'"

The young man said the instructor told him "we can handle that. I'm not going to let you give in to fear."

He said his first presentation was a nightmare, shaky knees and all. And then it got progressively easier. Class members were encouraged to talk about personal incidents, "things you are familiar with. We all pulled for each other and that literally helped pull all of us through," the young man said.

"But no one pulled for us like Mike. He's got to be one of the most dedicated people I've ever seen. I'll never forget him for what he has done for me and the others.

AS SPEAKER AFTER SPEAKER stood up and gave his or her interesting talk with apparent ease and clarity, our son leaned over and said: "You should have seen us 14 weeks ago. We were a bunch of nervous wrecks."

It was difficult to believe these poised, confident individuals had only recently been afraid to speak on their feet.

But week after week of encouragement and guidance by Mike Wilson, graduate assistants and a supportive audience of fellow classmates had gotten them out of their dark shell into the bright light of confidence.

"We pulled for each other, and here we are," said our son. Another son, also an invited guest, beamed proudly at his orator brother. "I knew you could do it," he said. "I had the same kind of fear you had at the beginning of the course."

His brother said, "Yes, but mine was laced with terror."

They recalled that during school they had few qualms about making a talk, but had developed a hangup on public speaking somewhere down the line.

Toward the end of the course, some had reservations about speaking to a larger group which included numerous invited guests at the graduation. By now they were used to their friendly and supportive audience.

But Mike Wilson assured them they could handle that. In fact, he said, it was easier to address a larger group. They would see.

So when one after the other of the Carnegie graduates confidently got to his or her feet and proudly stood ground while articulating to the much larger audience, Mike Wilson's smile got bigger and bigger. He was the personification of the father figure.

"Look at Mike," our son said, "you'd think he was getting a million dollars."

I couldn't help watching this remarkable man as I glanced from speaker to him and then back to speaker. What a coach he would have made with that ability to motivate.

But when I saw the pride on the faces of those formerly reluctant and nervous speakers I was glad Mike had kept his coaching where it could do the most good. This was more important.

THE GRADUATION BANQUET, ceremony and speaking took a few hours, and I got to bed four hours later than usual. But this time it was all right with me.

I felt great when I got up the next morning. I was still riding a high crest from the excitement of that great evening.

It's thrilling enough to watch your own son cross a threshold of fear and conquer it, but when you were privileged to witness others do the same, well, that was heady stuff.

And it wasn't just the fact the world now has X number more people who are capable of standing on their feet and speaking before an audience without shaking or fainting.

Here are people who have proved to themselves they can overcome fear. Whether it is fear of public speaking or some other form of fear, they have convinced themselves it can be done.

Now they can use this success to build on other forms of success. Success is even more contagious than fear, and they are living proof.

Mike Wilson, a former Navy fighter pilot, had prepared these fledglings for their solo flight.

And they had all skillfully landed on their feet.

IT'S LEGAL:
'THAT DOESN'T MAKE IT RIGHT'

I DON'T RECALL FORMALLY discussing ethics with my father. That is, there was not the formality of "let's sit down and talk" about how people should treat each other. What they should or should not do.

He was too busy and such preachy verbosity was not his style.

Yet, I couldn't help but learn about ethics just by being near this "man of his word" and by seeing how he dealt with people in all walks of life.

As I got older I could sense there was something special about my father because of the way others reacted. Although he was not a stuffed shirt and had a keen sense of humor, people treated him with much deference. It was the way he carried himself and talked and listened and respected the feelings of others.

What he got in return was an abundance of respect. I remember how impressed I was when he and I walked into a bank and there was a chorus of "Hello, Mr. Parker" and "How are you, Mr. Parker?"

At the time I thought this warm greeting was because my father had a large amount of money in that usually cold and austere bank. There were others who had much more. The bankers were greeting a man they respected and whose word was his bond.

He was not just a good businessman. He was a good man who happened to be in business and didn't believe you had to gouge anyone or deceive anyone in order to get ahead.

"You don't have to go after money with blood in your eyes," he would say.

I HAVE A FEELING that a great amount of empathy and sympathy for others was handed down to a youngster by the way his father treated those who were trying to feed and clothe their family with barely any means of income.

He didn't say, "Now son, these are good, hard-working people who barely have enough to live on from day to day, and I consider it not only my duty but my privilege to help them as much as possible."

But I saw and heard what went on, and I heard words of encouragement for those who had gone much too long without working. I also heard how he responded when a customer told him "I've got a job." "That's wonderful," he said, without asking what kind of a job the lucky customer had found in a country packed with millions of jobless.

I also recall how he extended credit far beyond the current earning or paying power of the customer. "He's a good man. When he finds work, he will pay his bill."

"Meanwhile," he was told, "you've got a bunch of customers who owe you money. How long can you keep this up?"

"As long as we can make a living from customers who have jobs."

He was optimistic "things will get better." Meanwhile, weren't we lucky we had an income and could pay our bills and were able to help some fine people who were out of work?

There were customers who had been carried on the books so long they were embarrassed.

I recall this vignette: "Isn't that Mr. Smith crossing the street and walking down to the store on the corner?" someone asked.

My dad said it was and that he knew why Mr. Smith had not been coming in to our store. "He owes us a big bill and he's afraid to come in."

"I don't blame him," was the reply.

"Neither do I," said my father, but they were coming from two different directions.

THE NEXT TIME my dad saw Mr. Smith walking past our store on the opposite side of the street, he motioned for him to stop by as he called out his name.

"Doesn't he owe you enough already?" my dad was asked.

Adding to the already big bill was not what my father had in mind. The conversation with Mr. Smith went something like this:

"Mr. Smith, you haven't been coming by the store lately."

"No, Mr. Parker. I owe you too much money already."

"But where do you buy your groceries now?"

"Down the corner at Mr. Brown's store."

"Does Mr. Brown give you credit?"

"No sir. I pay cash for the groceries I buy from him."

"So, if you're going to pay cash why not come in and trade with me. I can also use the cash."

The customer told my father he owed him "so much money" he didn't think my father wanted him to trade at his store.

My father assured him he would be most welcome and that if it would make him (the customer) feel any better, he could pay him a small amount of money every now and then just to trim down the credit account.

The customer agreed and was all smiles. So was my father, who instinctively knew how to deal with people and how to help them save their hard-pressed dignity and self-respect.

There was something about the way Sam Parker trusted and took a chance on people that was a beautiful thing to see.

MY FATHER WAS an optimist. This helped explain why he put so much trust in others and naturally he expected to be trusted.

Besides the two grocery stores he operated, he also liked to delve in modest real estate transactions.

On one occasion he phoned a real estate agent to tell him he would buy a certain piece of property. I believe it was on a Friday. The agent wanted him to come by his office that day so he could sign the papers and close the deal.

My dad told him he was too busy to do that, but he'd be by early Monday morning. I don't know what the agent said, but I remember my dad saying:

"Look, I told you I'd buy it. If you can't take my word for it, I don't want it."

The agent took his word for it and the paper transaction was finalized on Monday. A "word" was very important to my father.

On another occasion my dad was so impressed with a large parcel of property that he wanted to show it to one of his best friends.

He took his friend to the choice property he was eager to buy. "Isn't that a beauty?" would have been a typical question for this man who also enjoyed the success of others.

In turn, he expected others not to begrudge him what success he might achieve. That's the way he was.

So, how did he feel when his "friend" bought that property out from under him.

For a day or two he literally grieved. I recall my mother urging him not to take it so hard. She assured him there would be other good buys and to forget this deal he had lost.

"It's not just the property," he said. "I've also lost a friend."

HERE ARE SOME other lessons learned from his do-as-I-do ethics course:

My father was sparing in his criticism of others, but when I referred to a widely known individual as "a nice man," he set me straight.

"I don't think so," he said. "He takes advantage of people when he makes them loans."

"But is he operating legally?" I asked.

"That's not the point here. You can ruin a man and do it legally," he replied. "You can put him and his family out on the street and it may be legal, but that doesn't make it right."

This is the man who put mustard on handout bologna sandwiches "because it will taste better" for the hobos and other unemployed of the Great Depression.

He helped numerous people start their own business and offered encouragement along the way.

He tried to give salesmen an order as quickly as possible, even if it meant having a customer wait a few minutes. Another grocer questioned this practice. He explained:

"It only takes a few minutes. But if the salesman has to wait a long time in every store, it will be midnight before he gets home."

He insisted on instilling a strong work ethic in his son. I'm glad he did although at the time I frowned at going to work in the dark and getting off late at night. This was during school vacation.

He treated a poor man with as much dignity as a rich man.

And he wasn't impressed with the rich man if he took advantage of people. He liked most people but didn't like sham and "put on" and people who didn't have "a word."

When times were tough, he worked that much harder and his great sense of humor helped soften the bumps. He and my mother were a team long before women's rights.

One of his great friendships was with my wife's father, Selig Korenthal. They were close friends and had much in common character-wise. My father would assure his friend he was going to do well, and when his friend's business started to thrive it was hard to tell which of the two was the more delighted.

I got to know my father much better when I came back from overseas service in the Army. He wasn't as husky and stocky as he used to be. His health was failing. Thank God we became closer. We even became friends.

I miss the man. I miss my father.

'Class Act':
A Tough Act To Follow

Little Eddie Jenkins had class — with a capital "C" — in the third grade. He had it throughout his school days. It was more than just popularity. It was class, and it's hard to define except to say it is a form of elegance a person is practically born with. You either have it, or you don't.

I don't ever recall Eddie saying a malicious word about anyone. And he didn't cull his friends. They came from all walks of life, and he was just as comfortable being seen with the school's nerdiest nerd as he was talking to the top jock hero.

Maybe that's why everyone felt so comfortable and safe around Eddie. He also felt secure enough to be friendly with those his friends snubbed. Eddie didn't play that game.

He wasn't afraid it would damage his ego and reputation to be friendly with anyone he liked, regardless of how they stood in the pecking order. Everyone liked and respected Eddie. He had class.

General Weislogel was a West Pointer with more than his share of brains, drive and charisma. But, if I had to put one distinctive label on this unusual individual, I'd say he had class.

Forget those stars on his shoulders, if you could, although

they commanded attention and were more than enough to get the job done.

However, one of the things about General Weislogel that you noticed right away was the laid-back, comfortable way he handled his almost awesome power. He was personally interested in those around him and this interest extended to officer and enlisted man alike.

His was one of the finest class acts I ever witnessed during my five years of army service. The general was a textbook on how to use power without abusing it.

This translated into knowing how to get the best out of his officers and troops with the least amount of wear and tear on their nerves and egos.

He operated under the assumption: If you take away a soldier's pride and sense of self-importance, you have very much diminished that man's value to his outfit. He believed in preserving the dignity of the individual and allowing him room for initiative, not a standard operational procedure for the army.

Those who worked for and with the general must have been some of the finest soldiers in this man's army. They were the proudest individuals I ever met, and I was on numerous cadres which helped to train green troops.

The men respected him as an individual and as a general. They didn't fear him because they knew he was a humane and fair person who did not need to intimidate those around him as proof of his powerful position.

And yet the general had the reputation throughout his division as the one who could get the job done.

I hope I haven't given you a picture of an "I love everybody" type of individual without any temper, fire or displeasure in his makeup. That was not the case.

General Weislogel could get out of kilter, but he was always in control, in charge, and he was unflaggingly conscious of the worth and dignity of the officers and soldiers around him.

And yet there was nothing patronizing in his attitude. When you worked with the general, you knew you were working for a man who wanted to be surrounded by proud men, men with a strong sense of personal identity, not just robots.

General Weislogel was a great class act. One of the greatest. He left a profound impression.

With him, we felt we were winners even before we won the war!

A YOUNGSTER in the seventh grade, the first year of junior high school, "wasn't too good in math but liked to write themes."

He said, "My English teacher assigned us some homework. I forget the subject, but I jumped right into it because I liked to write."

He said he thought he had done a good job on the assignment, but that it backfired on him.

"Instead of giving me a good grade she told me she wanted to talk to me after class.

"When the others had gone she asked me who had helped me with the essay. I told her I didn't have any help with it. I didn't go into the fact my folks were from the Old Country and weren't that well-versed in English."

But the teacher wasn't convinced the work was his alone, and she told him she was not only disappointed he got help but also that he wouldn't admit it.

He left the classroom in a state of emotional disarray. "For one thing," he said, "she was a beautiful, blonde lady and I had a schoolboy crush on her. When she talked to me the way she did, it really hurt me. I couldn't understand why she didn't believe me."

At the time he also didn't understand the significance of a

pop essay that the teacher a few days later called on her class to write, in class.

He now understands.

"I think we had about 15 or 20 minutes in which to write it. Again, I don't remember the subject, but I remember the incident as if it were last week."

The following day his English teacher again asked him to stay after class. "I thought, oh no. Now what is she going to fuss at me about."

This time it was different. "She looked at me with those beautiful, gray-blue eyes and she said: 'I want to apologize to you for doubting you. I'm so sorry. Will you forgive me?'"

He said, "I could have sworn there were tears in her eyes. This was the first time in my life that anyone, especially a grownup, and a teacher at that, had apologized to me.

"I got an 'A' for my essay, but the main thing I was happy about was my teacher believed me. I also fell back in love with her."

This little drama took place in Mrs. Baird's seventh-grade class.

To my way of thinking, hers was a great class act.

AS A YOUNG REPORTER I was covering a U.S. Senate Rackets Committee hearing in Washington. The committee had named Robert Kennedy to head its investigation.

It was my first trip to Washington and just the logistics of finding my way around was enough to remind me I was working in a bigger league.

Luck would have it that Charlie Bartlett was a close friend of Robert and Jack Kennedy, and I knew the Pulitzer Prize-winning journalist when he worked for a while in Chattanooga earlier in his career.

Charlie had since gone on to Washington, won the coveted award and had become syndicated. A lot of things had happened to this fine reporter, but becoming swell-headed was not one of them.

Almost immediately after I saw Charlie, he asked me:

"Have you met Bobby Kennedy?" I told him I hadn't but would appreciate an introduction. This way I would get information that would give my reporting more depth.

He was not obligated to go out of his way for me. After all, journalism is a competitive business and he was also covering the Rackets Committee. But Charlie asked where I was staying and if there was anything else he could do to help.

"By the way," he said, "there's a press conference scheduled for 10 o'clock in the morning and it could produce some good copy."

I thanked him for his help and drove on back to my hotel.

I was there less than an hour before the phone rang. It was Charlie Bartlett. And in his fast-clipped way of speaking he told me:

"I just wanted you to know that they've changed the time of the conference. It'll be at 8 instead of 10. I didn't want you to miss it and think I had purposely given you the wrong time."

I thanked him again for being the class act he is and set my clock much earlier. Someone else wouldn't have been that helpful in the first place. And then to call to make sure I didn't miss the conference. He didn't have to do that.

But that's precisely why people with class stand out head and shoulders above the crowd. They are a different breed. An elegant breed.

After all of these years, when I think of Charlie Bartlett, I think of a guy with impeccable character and much class.

THE ATTRACTIVE LADY had recently undergone surgery. She seems to be doing fine and when she showed up at the office she was warmly welcomed by friends and colleagues.

In acknowledgement, she bravely beamed her dazzling high-kilowatt smile.

One of the welcomers especially empathized with her. His daughter had also had a bout with cancer but now seems to be back on the road to good health. The daughter has shown class in the upbeat way she has handled this setback.

For the first time in his life, he has also undergone numerous tests and doctor visits. He hasn't handled his and his daughter's situations too well. It has not been the best of times.

"Welcome back," he told the lady with the brave, beautiful smile. "We missed you."

"Thank you," she said as she squeezed his hand. "You and I have had quite a year. But now we're back."

Concern for others? This lady has CLASS spelled with big capital letters.

THE DICTIONARY DESCRIBES "class act" as "outstanding quality or prestige."

With this definition in mind we include those who engage in acts of kindness and consideration. But there are other nuances:

The millionaire who talked unashamedly and with pride about the humble origin of his family.

The colleague who returned $100 to a bank teller because "I didn't want her to have to make up the difference."

The bosses and parents who realized the importance of pride and self-esteem in the lives of employees and children.

Those who are in positions of power but don't abuse same. Those who respect the talents and intelligence of others.

The teacher who gave a non-speaking role as "king" to a

student because the child was in a stammering phase.

The wife of a boorish husband. She maintained her good-natured, pleasant disposition during many trying years.

Those who devote years of their lives uncomplainingly taking care of a sick wife or husband or some other member of the family.

The waitress, who bites her tongue and far outclasses the loud-mouth who has been giving her a hard time.

Those who take a chance on others and those who put themselves in the shoes of others.

Here's to all of you "class act" people. You are a tough act to follow.

A Tribute To
An Old Warrior

I'VE LOST ONE OF MY BEST AND OLDEST FRIENDS.

It so happened he was also the publisher for whom I have worked since 1947. But Roy McDonald, better known as Mr. Roy, was much more than that to me. He was also a friend, a colleague and a confidant.

His world was that of the daily newspaper. A fierce but fair competitor, he gloried in the day-to-day challenge of this exciting business and in being "where the action is." He had a knack for hiring key people who also loved the action of a hectic, fast-paced business. And how could they complain about unusual and long hours when their publisher habitually put in 70- to 80-hour work weeks?

No, he wasn't trying to make the Forbes 500 list. To him the challenge was the name of the game, not just the bottom line dollar figure. Operating a financially successful paper was just a way of keeping score. He loved this business and had a hands-on knowledge of every phase of its operation.

He once told me, "I'd build a penthouse on this building, but my wife, Elizabeth, wouldn't stand for it."

MR. ROY STOOD FOR a lot of things, including love of family and country and devotion to his God and church. He also stood for fairness and it is reflected in the newspaper's coverage. "We report the news, we don't make it. We go after the news; we don't go after people," he emphasized.

More than anyone I've ever known, he took to heart the Bible's admonition to do good deeds but to do them in a private, unheralded way. He shrugged off this charitable, compassionate trait as the normal thing to do.

"I've been down that same road," he said. "I know how it feels to get help when you really need it." As he usually did when making a point, he'd look over the top rims of his glasses for emphasis.

He could also be uncomfortably straight to the point, but you always knew how you stood with him. Mr. Roy would give you his undivided attention, but when he thought he had all the information he needed, you knew it. He would simply swing his chair completely around to his ever-present calculator and typewriter and literally be BACK to putting out a newspaper.

MR. ROY WAS IN THE BUSINESS of publishing and selling newspapers, but he devoted an incredible amount of time in giving of his self, his limitless energy, his wisdom and an enormous amount of quietly-given help to countless people, many of whom fitted the underdog category.

His enthusiasm for work and the newspaper business was shared by those with whom he surrounded himself. His prodigious working habits were legendary as well as his zest for accepting life's challenges.

The man was a born optimist and as with most entrepreneurs, he had a proclivity for taking chances. However, his razor-sharp business acumen ensured that the chances would be calculated risks. "You win some and you lose some," he observed. Luckily for him and for us, he won more than he lost. Much more.

He was loyal to a fault, and this sort of old-fashioned loyalty rubbed off on those who worked for and with him. If you praised our friend, the publisher, we agreed you were perceptive. If you criticized him, you were treading on thin ice with us. But aren't friends — even those who happen to be publishers — supposed to be defended, especially when they are unique and exceptionally deserving?

Many here at the paper knew the soft and compassionate side of this tough old warrior. He might raise his high-pitched voice another octave or two as he chided a young family man for "getting into this kind of a financial mess," and then proceed to completely bail him out of his predicament.

Mr. Roy couldn't handle effusive "thanks" too well, however sincere it might be. On those numerous occasions when amazed recipients gratefully thanked him, he'd mumble "all right, all right" and turn back to his calculator — not that he really needed one.

He had his own built-in mental computer. The man was a mathematical marvel, having sharpened his basic math while working for his grocer father and then later in his own chain of groceries.

OUR PUBLISHER WAS A DYNAMO of energy and whoever coined the phrase "taking care of business" must have had him in mind. At any given time he knew what was going on throughout his beloved paper.

The fact that those who worked for him also knew that he knew certainly didn't cut down on productivity and the meeting of deadlines. As one admiring employee observed: "He's all over the place."

Yet, his office door was always open to the public, whether it was a frail elderly lady or gentleman wanting to recall "those Home Store days" or a highly placed civic leader or elected official. He was as much at ease with the famous as with the common man.

"Come on in," was the friendly welcome. Thousands did over the years and enjoyed his finely-honed wit and his tremendous ability to remember facts long since forgotten by lesser mortals.

He was one of the best storytellers I have ever heard. No matter the occasion, he could come up with an appropriate gem to illustrate the point, and it would hit the target.

Roy McDonald had a mind like a steel trap. Once information was acquired, it was forever retained. Although the years had slowed him physically, mentally he was as sharp and alert as ever, up to the day he died.

His cluttered desk would have been the dismay of an efficiency expert, but there was nothing cluttered about his mind. Besides, he knew what was on top, in the middle of and at the bottom of that enormous pile of papers and pictures. His secretaries claimed he could tell if anything had been removed and "filed."

He had his own filing system. Everything about this "original" was unique, including his daring achievements. He felt if he could perceive it, he could achieve it. His was such a strong will and personality that we all found ourselves believing he could . . . and he did.

He had no awe of the famous or of rank. In turn, he didn't have to pull rank in order to get things done. If Mr. Roy wanted it, Mr. Roy got it.

WHEN I GOT out of the Army in 1945, I became a partner in a beverage business and did quite well. Later, I was a partner in a chenille-robe manufacturing business and was almost disrobed.

I made money in one of the businesses. In the other, I found out what can happen when styles, tastes and new machinery come into play. But from both ventures I learned that running a business can be a headache and is not the panacea it is cracked up to be.

In school, I remembered, I always enjoyed English, literature and writing themes much more than mathematics and science. Why not put this penchant to use as a livelihood? With this in mind, I called on Publisher Roy McDonald with the help of an introduction by Bill Hagan, who later became a city editor.

Bill warned me there were no openings, but he said he would introduce me if I insisted. The publisher, as Bill had predicted, told me at least a half-dozen times there were no openings. I insisted at least that many times he'd be making a mistake if he didn't hire this eager beaver.

He told me I wouldn't make the kind of money I made in business, and I wouldn't be satisfied. I thought to myself I also wouldn't lose the kind of money I lost in the chenille venture.

I persisted. I wanted to be a reporter. He tried to steer me to the advertising section of the paper. I hung in there.

Finally, he asked: "You've been in business. What's the biggest problem you had?

Not knowing anything about the publisher's philosophy or ideology, I replied: "Getting 60 minutes of work for 60 minutes of pay."

He smiled: "Throw your hat on the rack and go to work."

Bill Hagan was surprised when I told him I had been hired. "Where am I going to put you?" he asked.

Wherever it was, it's exactly where I have enjoyed being all of these years — where the action is.

That's where my publisher friend has always enjoyed being. Life goes on, and hopefully I'll still be doing my job for some time to come. But with Mr. Roy gone, there'll be a vital piece of the "action" missing.

THIS HAS NOT BEEN a kind year.

This past week we lost a great friend and publisher. Mr. Roy was a giant in the newspaper field. His death marks the end of an era. There will never be another like him. I will never have another friend like him. I'll always miss him.

He was not only our publisher, but in his own inimitable way, he was a father figure for many of us.

"Son," he once told a young reporter, "you're worrying too much. No one is perfect. After you've done the best you can do, quit worrying. Use your energy for something constructive."

Roy McDonald always did the best he could do and his best was history-making in the newspaper world he loved. He also did his best for family, friends and colleagues. We join thousands in mourning his death.

Now those at his newspaper who worked for him so loyally and enthusiastically will honor this great man by continuing to do their best.

So long, old warrior. Rest in the peaceful bosom of your beloved farm, away from the sights and sounds and fray of battle.

You were one of a kind and seemed so invincible we thought you'd always be here with us.

Rest peacefully, dear friend. You've earned it.

ONE OF THE WORLD'S
TOUGHEST JOBS

PEOPLE MANAGEMENT HAS GOT to be one of the most difficult and interesting jobs in the world.

Almost everyone manages something on a day-to-day basis. This is often important, technical and demanding work. But those who are successful in the people-managing business have an added dimension of challenge and excitement: Their paths are literally strewn with emotional landmines that at any given moment could hurt and damage personnel and company.

"Here's the picture," said a successful, middle-management executive. "My job is to see that the job gets done. If it doesn't, I'm the one who is held responsible. I get the blame first and then it is passed down the line."

He said he probably makes his job tougher on himself by not taking an autocratic or intimidating approach. "I try to treat people the way I'd like to be treated and that sometimes creates a problem. There are always a few who will attempt to take advantage, but of course this can be dealt with."

He believes his policy of "respecting the individual" encourages initiative and production. "It not only helps the person to retain a high opinion of himself but benefits the company in the long run."

A PERSON WHO IS WORTH hiring is "worth being given a chance to show what he or she can do without being hemmed in too much.

"I've seen people blossom forth when given additional responsibility and backed by the confidence of higher-ups. It's remarkable what people can do when they are given the challenge and some freedom to use their own talent."

The manager said, "If you continually treat a person as if he doesn't have sense enough to think for himself, such a person may start acting that way. You are hurting the person's usefulness to the company because you are hurting him in his own estimation."

He said he encourages people to make individual decisions whenever possible "because that shows they are thinking." Naturally, he would expect those decisions to generally coincide with company policy. "But sometimes an unusual idea can change policy.

"Companies and corporations must feel that employee-management relationships are very important. Why else would they have so many clinics and sessions on the subject?"

But, he said, he is amazed "at the lack of basic understanding of human relations" on the part of those who ought to know better. "Plain common sense should tell you people will be happier and more productive in their work if they are treated with respect and dignity than if they are spurred, browbeaten and intimidated.

"I'm talking about most people," he qualified.

THE MANAGER SAID there are many factors other than "fair salaries" that encourage on-the-job happiness.

"I wish I had a thousand dollars for each time I've heard

someone gripe about something that was bugging him." He added, "I also wish I had a thousand dollars for the good it did that person to get the gripe off his chest. Most of the time that was all he wanted. Most people are realistic enough to realize when something can or cannot be changed."

What surprises him, he said, is the lack of communication in some offices and businesses. "The most successful operations are those whose doors are always open to anyone in the organization.

"The opinions of others are important. Some companies become inbred and sterile because they don't want any input except at the very top. Failure to keep open a line of communication with employees is obviously not a healthy procedure."

Other things that surprise this human relations practitioner:

"Failure to give credit when due. There are too many who will quickly criticize but who fail to balance constructive criticism with an occasional pat on the back, if it is deserved. Adults and kids respond to sincerely meant praise. Most people need more than adequate or good pay. They need job satisfaction."

THE PEOPLE MANAGER, who uses a "down-to-earth approach" to his job, also stressed the need for "consistency and fairness" in dealing with people.

"There is hardly anything that will cause disruption as surely as showing undue favoritism or in being inconsistent or unrealistic in your demands. Riding a good horse into the ground doesn't make any sense at all. Unfortunately there are some who will do that just because they are in a position of authority. That is too bad. Such a person causes harm to people and to the organization."

He said people with responsible jobs must expect "a certain amount of pressure since the job in itself will bring it on. A skillful people manager will try to ease the pressure by his demeanor, a smile or words of assurance and praise and by keeping the criticism to a minimum.

"He will try to take the sting out of criticism and not be too quick or eager to criticize. He will let it slide on occasion. And even if something stupid has taken place, he will try to separate the person from the act. The person may have had a lapse which allowed something stupid to happen. But never call that person 'stupid.'"

Is advice this obvious and basic really necessary for those in positions of management?

"You'd be surprised," said the people manager. His advice also applies to the broader spectrum of human relations. It pertains to parents and teachers, to married couples and to most inter-personal relationships.

Pick out the person who seems to stay in a constant state of emotional disarray. He is short-fused and quick to blame those around him for his unhappiness. In a way he is right. This person has failed to learn one of the most important things in life: The art of getting along with others.

And for some flukish reason — because life plays such tricks — such an uptight one sometimes winds up in a position of management. Others then become the targets for his temper tantrums and his down-in-the-mouth moodiness.

This type of "manager," who has never learned to manage his own moods and feelings, can wreak havoc in an office or company. In his eagerness to "get the job done," he rides roughshod over anyone he views as an obstacle. His idea of motivation is to intimidate. He is not concerned about the individual as such. You do it his way, or else.

Unfortunately, this intemperate behavior is often overlooked by upper management, which is more interested in not making waves than in the emotional health of their employees. They are so busy looking at "the bottom line" they overlook the fact that human resources basically make the difference in the annual report.

Not All Winners
Wear The 'Gold'

"YOU WIN SOME and you lose some," he said. "That's why you've got to take time and appreciate the ones you win. How else are you going to enjoy winning?"

This advice comes from a gentleman who has "been around longer than most" and who has picked up many pointers on how the game should be played and enjoyed.

If you had to describe him in black and white terms with no grays thrown in, you'd definitely label him a winner. He has all the hallmarks including enthusiasm, an undaunted zest for living and confidence without arrogance.

At what point did he realize he was going to be a winner in the game of life and business?

He replied, "After I'd been knocked around more times than I care to remember. I wasn't proud of those failures, but I started feeling good about myself for having the guts to keep fighting back.

"That," he said, "is what separates winners from losers if I might immodestly point out."

He added, "What I'm saying is that if you live long enough, you're going to get your share of lumps. This happens to all of us. But all people don't react the same. Some just figure what's the use of trying and so they give up. They don't even give

153

themselves a second chance, much less a third, fourth, fifth."

Changing metaphors, he said it stands to reason "the more times you're up to bat, the better chance you have of getting a hit. Too many people are afraid of striking out. They'd rather not play the game than go down swinging. That's too bad. They'll never know what their full potential might have been. They just don't have the heart for the game."

WHY ARE SOME PEOPLE so determined to be winners that they are willing to take painful lumps and bruises to keep fighting until they've won?

"It all has to do with motivation," he said. "We all need a certain amount of brains and luck, but motivation, determination is what drives you on. If you don't have the desire, the drive to win, you're not going to win.

"Ask any football coach and hear what he tells you about players who aren't as good athletes as others, but who outplay the others because of their intense desire to win."

Is motivation spurred on by pride and self-esteem, family consciousness or other factors?

"A lot of things, including the ones you mention, go into motivation and ambition. It depends on the individual. But I'll tell you one thing that will light the fire under you: Be born into a family during the Depression days and spend most of your time being at least half hungry and doing odd jobs while trying to figure out how to get by from one day to the next."

He said, "With that kind of a start, if you've got any drive at all, you'll try to make sure you won't have to go through that kind of thing again, even if the bottom should fall out of the economy which it won't do again . . . not like before.

"I wonder," he added, "if we really do our children a big favor by leaving them a lot of money and making things too easy for them."

He said he had seen what happens to young people who are brought up in a hot-house, insulated world and haven't had or didn't want the opportunity to try and fail on their own.

"They haven't been tempered by the heat of struggle or competitiveness and in the back of their minds is the thought that someday they'll come into a fortune.

"These are the ones," he said, "who had better be careful that some guy who had been a streetwise kid scratching for a living doesn't take them to the cleaners.

"I don't say there is anything great or romantic about having a poor beginning, but, oh boy, you sure can learn from it. It can motivate the heck out of you if you're a fighter."

AFTER ALL OF THESE YEARS, he admits he still gets choked up at genuine displays of courage, fortitude and high ideals.

"The other day I was watching a show about athletes who just barely missed winning their gold medal four years ago at the Olympics. Each one had a touching story to relate, and described how close they were to winning the gold. One lost by a centimeter.

"But the one who got to me the most was a young man who was told his sister had died back home in the United States just a few hours before his event. He said he tried to tell himself he should win the race for her, that she would have wanted it that way, but he was in a state of semi-shock and couldn't fully concentrate on his event."

The news had cost him a gold medal.

"His mother was in the talk-show audience and she was asked why the family didn't keep the sad news to itself until after her son had his chance to be a winner.

"She replied they were a close-knit family and he would have found out from press dispatches and he especially wouldn't have wanted to find out that way."

Then the young man was asked if the news of his sister's death shouldn't have been kept from him for a while. He replied that as important as the Olympic Games are to him, they are just games.

"I loved my sister," the athlete said. "This is a human life we are talking about. She is more important to me than any Olympics could ever be."

The athlete's admirer added, "How do you like that for wisdom and a sense of priorities at a young age?"

And from one winner to another: "That young man got to me. I mean he really got to me. He lost that gold medal but what a winner he is. A real winner!"

They Can 'Light A Fire' Under You

A BRUISER OF A FOOTBALL player was being interviewed following a close win over a rival college. He had been selected as one of the key players of the game, having made two of his team's three touchdowns.

As expected he gave his blocking teammates the credit for his sensational runs and then he had this to say about his coach:

"He's not only a fine coach who teaches you the basics of the game and expects you to give 100 percent effort, but he also wants you to play the game right and he expects you to do what's right on the field and off the field.

"The man cares about you as a person, not just as a football player. He makes sure you know right from wrong, and if you don't, you're not going to play football for him."

The player emphasized the importance his coach attached to "personal values" and to integrity.

"He's made a big difference in my life," he said with considerable feeling.

EVEN AS HE SPOKE I felt I knew where he was coming from: A home where certain basic values weren't stressed. Why else would this 20-year-old be so impressed with a successful formula for life that should have been given him as a youngster?

Better late than never. But parents (most importantly) and many non-value teaching instructors had apparently failed to do their job.

How then had this fine athlete succeeded to this point in his career?

Because he had something going for him called talent. And there must have been a better than average sense of personal identity and deep-down pride that made him want to "amount to something."

He was lucky. But how about those who have nothing to keep them going, neither talent nor pride nor a sense of values instilled by parents who also had a strong sense of values?

Unless one is unusually strong willed or unusually talented, lack of proper parental support and nurturing will keep that person from becoming a key player in whatever game he or she chooses.

Key player? Without the motivation of parents who care and instill value systems which work in our society, this kind of person won't even be able to get in the "game."

And then if teachers and others don't bother to help pull up the slack and explain the do's and don't's of the game — to do what's right — this kind of "player" will become "ineligible" for life.

He won't tackle and he certainly won't carry the ball for a touchdown or for any other kind of success in the game of life.

AND THERE IS Tue Nguyen, who just nine years ago arrived in this country with thousands of other Vietnamese boat people.

To say this 26-year-old is eager to learn and succeed is a gross understatement. He has already earned his seventh degree from the Massachusetts Institute of Technology, a doctorate in nuclear engineering.

He was described as a person with great willpower and determination "to get the most out of my time at MIT and out of my tuition."

Granted, this young man is most unusual. Even MIT concedes his accomplishments in the above time frame are a record.

But his brothers also aren't wasting their time. Taien Nguyen, 25, is also earning a doctorate in nuclear engineering at MIT, and Tai Nguyen, 22, is doing graduate work at the University of California at Berkeley.

Now they seem to be in the enviable position of being able to write their own ticket for the future.

But nine years ago the brothers spent three days at sea squeezed into a small boat with 300 other refugees. They arrived in Malaysia and spent nine months in a refugee camp.

They were literally rescued by a church group which sponsored their passage to Pasadena, Texas, where they moved in with relatives.

As miserable as life is for millions of poor and disadvantaged citizens of our country, how many would have been willing to be in that sea-swamped boat and in the refugee camp?

And how many would jump at the chance for education as did Tue Nguyen and his brothers?

SO WHAT IS IT that motivates these and other Vietnamese? A Vietnamese counselor here in this city explains it this way:

"Not only is there a sense of personal pride but this pride extends to a feeling of family pride. We feel that if we work hard and receive honors, that we are also honoring our parents who have always urged us to better ourselves."

She added, "This feeling of pride in ourselves and family is encouraged by our parents. If we let our family down, we have let ourselves down. There is no separation of the two."

The counselor said her countrymen "are hungry for the opportunity to succeed" — for themselves and for their family.

We know where the boat people came from. We also know "where they are coming from" in regard to their ambition and a chance to be someone above average in this land of opportunity.

It is the opportunity to succeed that has motivated millions of new citizens from foreign shores. These people also came here without knowledge of the English language and with precious little means of support.

Yet, there was a willingness to work and to learn, with many of them attending night school so they could learn to read, write and speak better English in their adopted country, a country which allowed them the freedom to better themselves.

They also had a strong sense of pride in self and family. It is no coincidence that accomplishment and the nurturing of the family circle seem to be the formula for success.

Millions of people came over in ships and in boats and they came here from all over the world.

The statement, "I know where you're coming from," conveys much more than a place on the map.

PEOPLE REACT DIFFERENTLY to various situations and stimuli.

Being born poor and raised in poverty may literally destroy all ambition for some as they are pushed into the ground. On the other hand, poverty and hardship have been catalysts which have motivated those with ambition to become successful in a matter of a few years.

Some of the wealthiest people around are those who were

born "dirt poor" and who were determined they would rise above this humble circumstance.

A multimillionaire, who proudly recalled the struggle his parents had to feed and clothe a brood of six, had this to say:

"I believe that being born into a poor family can make you dream more and be more determined to have plenty of money some day. You remember those hard times, and you don't want your family to have to go through that.

"Being poor will either kill your ambition or light a fire under you," said this wealthy man.

We not only knew where he was coming from, we knew where his family came from — from a little village in Russia — and the most priceless treasure they could give him and his brothers was a strong sense of family love and support and pride in self and family.

They were never given a new car by doting parents, but they were instilled with the desire to succeed by parents who were poor in worldly goods but rich in spirit.

EDDIE IS A
'WORLD CHAMPION' DREAMER

A FEW YEARS AGO Eddie was considered to be a "real contender," a challenger in the boxing world. He was powerful and fast and "packed dynamite" in both fists.

Most of all, from the standpoint of screaming, action-hungry fans, he was a big drawing card because he was an exciting fighter to watch.

An old boxing aficionado described the ex-boxer this way:

"I'd say he was in the mold of a Jack Dempsey. He could box but he preferred to get in there and punch. Eddie was never in a dull fight in his life. He either knocked his opponent out or he went the distance. I don't ever remember the time he was knocked out.

"He had a cast-iron jaw and a heart of steel. The guy was always in good shape, and he never knew what it meant to quit or slow down in a fight, even if he was taking some hard licks. He never backed up. He was like a bulldog: You either annihilated him or he wouldn't turn you loose."

He said Eddie became a nationally ranked contender in the light-heavyweight division and at one time was listed in *Ring Magazine* as third in line for the crown. But he never quite made it to the very top.

"He kept telling everybody he was going to be the champ some day and there for a while it looked liked he might. But then he peaked and he started to slip year after year and never again was in a main event.

"He kept taking more and more punches but he was considered dangerous even after he became too old to have a chance. He was afraid of nobody.

"Finally the boxing commission refused to grant him a license, and that was one of the best things for his health, but it hurt him real bad emotionally.

"He became paranoid about it and claimed they wouldn't let him fight because some promoters had framed him since he refused to kick back half of his winnings."

He said he went along with this explanation because Eddie had a lot of pride and still dreamed of being champion some day.

NOT TOO LONG AGO Eddie came to the newspaper to get a reporter to do a story on him. He's still a big, impressive-looking individual who dresses rather nattily and uses a lot of cologne. You could envision him in the ring, beady eyes and cauliflower ears and all.

But the fellow who came up to the city desk had to try to speak above the office clatter since we had typewriters back then and not quiet word processors. His voice was a hoarse whisper, the result of too many blows to the Adam's apple.

He also walked with a round-heeled gait, the result of too many punches to the head. Putting it mildly, Eddie was more than a little punchy. But like the Eddie of old, the dangerous fighting machine that had been programmed to destroy opponents, he was still a dreamer. That's why he wanted to talk to a reporter.

"If he writes me up," said Eddie, "I can send the clipping to some big-time promoters in Chicago or New York and they can get me a match with the champ.

This time he wanted to fight the heavyweight champion because "I've put on about 30 pounds and I wouldn't want to try and make the lighter division because it would weaken me too much.

"Feel this arm," he whispered. "I'm as strong as I ever was."

He admitted he'd have to do a lot of road work in order to get his wind back. "I know I can beat him," he said. "This present crop of fighters ain't got the guts and stamina we had when I was fightin'. If I could just get a chance, I would win the title, and that's a fact."

WITH THAT STATEMENT of "fact," Eddie quickly looked to the left and then to the right, leaned closer and confided: "Do you know what the title is worth nowadays? I'd say it could make me a millionaire inside of a year."

I wondered how many years of fighting this 60-year-old warrior thought he had left. Apparently it never occurred to him that time was a tougher opponent than any opponent he ever faced in the ring.

A city editor saw him as more than a battered fighter who had illusions of grandeur. This was an individual with a dream that had been punched into fragments . . . and he was determined to put those shattered pieces back together again, time and missed opportunities notwithstanding.

I introduced Eddie to a young reporter and told the reporter to "just listen to him and see what he has to say." I said that maybe in a sense he is still a winner because he refused to take the count.

A human interest story came out of the interview, and as far as Eddie was concerned the reporter was a friend for life. The friendship was reciprocated.

HARDLY A COUPLE OF WEEKS went by that Eddie didn't drop in for a visit with the reporter who treated him with warmth, kindness and dignity.

I always thought highly of the talented and sensitive young reporter and his treatment of Eddie added to the accuracy of my estimation.

Once when Eddie was overheard telling the reporter he thought he had a match "lined up with Ali," some found it hard to keep a straight face. The reporter, who had to keep these visits short, made it clear to a couple of colleagues that Eddie was a "nice, gentle man" who was paying the price for being too fearless in the ring and didn't deserve to be snickered at.

No other stories were written about Eddie, but Eddie looked forward to his bimonthly newspaper visits. The reporter's touching consideration for the old fighter never flagged. When Eddie assured him the "match is almost lined up," the reporter said, "That's fine, I'm glad for you" or something equally reassuring.

And when Eddie dropped in at inopportune times, the reporter still treated him with kindness. It seemed Eddie understood what the term "deadline" meant. On one occasion when gently reminded of "deadline," Eddie said in his raspy whisper: "Get in there kid. Go get'em."

The young reporter liked the old fighter, and if he helped keep his dreams alive, where was the harm?

"I guess we all need dreams," said the reporter, "even those whose dreams will never come true."

Especially those.

THINGS HAVE A WAY of changing, and one day when Eddie inquired about his friend the reporter he was told he "no longer works here." Eddie was too good a fighter to telegraph his blows, but he made little effort to hide his disappointment.

"How can I get in touch with him?" he wanted to know. He stopped short of asking who was going to patiently and sympathetically listen to his "championship" match-ups.

Eddie left after he told me about some of his ethereal plans. No, the promoters hadn't answered his letter "yet," but he felt they would because "the new talent isn't too good, and they need a headliner like me to pull in the crowds.

"I'll be seeing ya," he said, with a gaptooth smile. "I'll let you know when I get that match lined up with Ali. I think the problem is he don't want no part of me. He's afraid I'll take him apart."

"Could be," I agreed.

EDDIE'S VISITS TO THE PAPER became less frequent. On several occasions I had to remind him that his reporter friend was no longer with us.

"That's right," he rasped. The old fighter then countered with, "I was hopin' he might have come back."

And then the visits stopped for almost a year until Eddie dropped in on us this past week. He had aged noticeably, and he wasn't as nattily dressed as usual. But he had a big, confident smile on his face that almost hid his beady little eyes.

"I'M A RICH MAN!" said Eddie. "I'VE WON FIVE MILLION DOLLARS. LOOK AT THIS."

He tenderly unfolded one of those numerous "millionaire sweepstakes" entries which are now making the rounds.

"Look," he whispered excitedly. "It says I've won $5 million. Now I can buy me some new clothes and a car and live in style."

Eddie had me on the horns of a dilemma. He was hallucinating again, but should I set him straight?

He answered the question for me when he asked: "Would you write them and get my check for me?"

"Eddie," I hedged, "you haven't won, yet. This is a contest in which there will be some winners, and it COULD be you, but not yet."

The smile vanished. "But it has got my name written here. See? And it also says I get a 'guaranteed income' each year."

I hated to be the one to tell Eddie that still another dream of his had taken the count.

No, he hadn't filled out anything. He had thrown "that other stuff away" when he thought he had already won the $5 million dollars.

On another occasion, Eddie said he hadn't sent a "winning" sweepstakes in because he was afraid "it might get lost in the mail."

Eddie never claimed he was an Einstein.

He does claim he can be the champion "if they'd just give me a chance."

THESE WILL BE THE 'GOOD OLD DAYS'

"HOW GOOD WERE the 'good old days' and what made them so good?"

The question was asked by a young man who was obviously ready to prove the best of days are right now and not fifty or sixty years ago. And considering his youth and vitality, no doubt he is right.

Fifty or sixty years from now he'll look back on these days as the good old days because they will be HIS good old days.

You ask me how good were my days, and I'll tell you they were mostly great.

What made them so great? The same thing that holds true for every generation: They were the vigorous, muscle-flexing days of our youth, plus the fact time and nostalgia have a way of eliminating much of the negative and accentuating the positive.

Never mind that my good old days were lacking the current technological breakthroughs in medicine, space and entertainment.When I was young I didn't spend much time worrying about doctors, annual checkups and the state of medical technology. For one thing, it seemed that youth and its vitality were ours to keep forever.

Youthful myopia also leads you to believe your parents will

always be with you. It comes as a shock to see their vulnerability as age backs them into a corner.

And when you are young in a different day and age and life is already heady and exciting, you don't need television, VCR's and Nintendo games to give spice to your life.

Youth has always drawn heavily on its imagination to entertain itself and to get itself into predicaments that cause consternation to parents.

WHAT DID I LIKE better about my growing up days, besides the fact I was much younger and practically pain-free except for an occasional stubbed toe?

Unlike many displaced modern youngsters, I liked the feeling of being part of a family unit, one that cared very much about me and was concerned about my future.

I liked someone to be proud of my small victories and to encourage me to succeed and point out pitfalls. I liked the fact I could count on my parents being at home.

I think I even liked the idea of neighbors also looking out for me even though at the time I thought they were mighty nosy.

A case in point: I was seen riding my new bike down steep Palmetto Street hill and across Oak Street without even slowing down for traffic.

After a warning and the second such transgression reported by a neighbor, my father made shambles of my bike. "Better this should happen to your bicycle than to you," he said as I watched in disbelief.

I liked my dedicated teachers who tried to ignite small sparks into flames of curiosity and made me want to learn.

Although I was not a straight "A" student, I developed a love for reading which many young television viewers now seem to lack. I may not have read *War and Peace* before I was 13, but I read my share of Tom Swift as well as detective and pirate books.

It didn't matter at the time. What mattered was I developed a taste for reading which brought my imagination into play. I recall the disappointment I experienced reading one particularly blood-curdling pirate book that had a picture of the chief scoundrel. He didn't look nearly as vicious and dastardly as the one I had conjured in my mind.

I liked radio and the music and shows in this magic box. One could listen to the wonderful invention and "see it on the radio" much as I saw my pirate villain in my mind's eye.

FOR A WHILE, I wondered why food tasted so much better in the good old days. Were the cooks and chefs so much better then? Was the food better? Not really, but our young taste buds were working on all their cylinders.

To this day I like ice cream. It is one of my strongest weaknesses. But I can recall the taste of an ice cream cone back then and the symphony of flavor and texture each lick of the cone produced.

They don't make ice cream the way they used to. That's what is said about many products. They also don't replace old taste buds for new ones. Not yet, anyway.

And then there were the movies. What difference did it make that some cynical, inbred movie critic hadn't recommended the movie you were now watching. Not much. If you enjoyed the movie, that was the name of the game. And you didn't need an "R" rating and four-letter words to enjoy it.

And when air-conditioning came into use and you were sitting in the arctic air of the Tivoli, it didn't matter what was on the screen. For a few cents you were in the lap of luxury.

Later, when you got a window air conditioner and even had

an air-conditioned car, you wouldn't swap with the crowned heads of Europe. Some drivers displayed signs which stated snobbishly: "This car is air-conditioned."

Before air conditioning, you accepted the fact that when you awoke in the morning you were drenched from the heat. It was summer, wasn't it?

Despite this, the good old days were also great because, being young, you could take this and hundreds of other inconveniences, including ants and flies at picnics, in stride. Noisy kids were also easier to take. Manners then were better as a rule than now.

Automobiles are much more complex than they were in those days. They are also more expensive compared to the worth of dollars then and now.

Seems cars back then didn't need to have as many repair jobs, either. And if you took it in for repair, you usually got it done on the day or hour it was promised.

Could it be that people took their promises more seriously?

LIFE WAS MUCH SIMPLER, the advocates of the good old days will tell you. And in many ways it was. Raising a family in a relatively drug-free society was less hazardous, as frightened families will now attest.

Filling out an income tax form was a snap. Cholesterol wasn't even a health factor and very few kids talked back to parents or teachers.

An examination by your family physician was not the involved and often scary procedure it is now and hardly anyone ever thought of suing him or any other friend.

He didn't have the benefit of modern medical know-how, but this exponent of caring and common sense had the power to make you worry less and place complete confidence in his expertise and concern for you. And from a psychological standpoint, the family physician was a miracle worker, since our minds also help us to heal.

Polio and other dreaded diseases were still taking their human toll. They have since been contained, but AIDS is the current scourge of a more promiscuous society, which even now is becoming more careful if not more moral.

Teachers and parents were high on our list of important persons during our formative years. The bad ones were noticeably bad; the good ones were great. They helped us over many hurdles.

FROM WHAT WE CAN determine, more emphasis is now placed on the importance of young people's psyches and self-confidence. There is more of an effort to consider the young individual's total needs and to understand all youngsters are not talented in the same way or degree.

There is also more inclination today to listen to the child and allow him certain rights. The other side of the coin is to take this too far, to the point where the child is giving the orders.

Some young parents are too interested in being friends with their children and not determined enough to assume the role of parent, which sometimes requires sterner measures, especially in regard to anti-social behavior.

The "do it because I say so" era of the "good old days" produced more discipline and better-behaved children. It did not make for individualism and inspire self-confidence.

However, even back then there were some parents ahead of their time. They also realized a child armed with self-confidence and proper discipline was better able to cope with the tough real world out there.

MORE OF THE GOOD and the not-so-good of then and now:

Informality is all right up to a point, and sometimes it is relaxing. But there are times when "getting dressed up" is proper and more fun for the occasion. Good manners should never go out of style. Back then we didn't have to worry about a wife or girlfriend being shocked by four-letter words at a movie, although many women now accept this as another fact of life. And the less explicit older movies romanticized relationships instead of exploiting them. More was left to the imagination.

When you had a date back then, you came into the house and met the girl's parents. Believe it, you didn't just blow the horn and wait for her to come running out. You also opened the door for your date, and she didn't feel insulted. Both of you wore shoes.

There was more emphasis placed on morals and manners and no one bragged about live-in relationships and having children out of wedlock. There was also hypocrisy, since human nature rarely changes.

There was more time to communicate in a television-less era and more people used their reading skills.

We were less of a throw-away society back then, especially in regard to friends and marriages. "For better or worse."

What's good about these days? They're here and so are we and we need to appreciate each and every one.

Besides, one of these days they'll be the "good old days."

BANNY: A TRIBUTE AND A TOUGH DECISION

BETTY'S MOTHER — BANNY — Mrs. Ida (Adele) Barnett, had asked, "Will I ever see you again?" as she prepared to fly back to Florida last May after a visit with us. We assured her she would see us in November when we intended to visit her.

She shook her head. She knew more than she had told us. But she seldom complained.

As it turned out, our visit came a month sooner when we learned she was in the hospital suffering from a heart condition. We drove to Hallendale and arrived at the hospital on the afternoon of the second day, October 5.

During those visits we could talk with her as she removed her oxygen mask time and again. And talk we did. There was no doubt in our minds as to who loved whom. This was no time for holding back, and we didn't. This dearest of ladies never held back in the love and affection she gave her family and to her friends, and we figured that turnabout was fair.

What wasn't fair was a decision we had to make the second night after our arrival. The doctor informed us that Banny was "slipping fast" and needed to be put on a respirator to keep her alive.

The usual questions: "What chances does she have without it?" The reply was "none."

"What are her chances with it?" The reply: "There is no guarantee."

Those few seconds seemed like an eternity as Betty and I weighed whether we should put Banny on a life-support machine. We had never seen one and a respirator sounded as if she would be given even more oxygen.

We agreed the doctor should ask Banny first. He told us later she shruggingly acquiesced to being hooked up to this mechanical roller coaster.

We doubt she would have agreed if she fully knew what was going to happen to her. In retrospect, Betty and I wonder if we did the right thing, considering what she went through and the fact her condition was essentially irreversible.

That night, with the respirator tube in her throat, Banny could no longer communicate with us except by a clutch and a squeeze of a hand. She tried desperately to talk but she could only mouth the words. There was a look of terror on her face we will never forget.

Time and again we asked ourselves: "Did we do the right thing?" How much of what we did was to salve our own conscience? And yet we felt if Banny had a chance, even an outside one, she should not be denied that chance.

The decision was one of the hardest we have ever made. It has caused us to seriously consider a "living will" whereby one previously determines the use of a respirator, an anesthetized word for a life-support system where the patient is hooked up to tubes that resemble a science-fiction nightmare.

"There is so much she wants to tell us," Betty said. "She is so frustrated because we can't understand her."

She tried writing, but she was too weak. Once in a while Betty would lip read and Banny would smile that beautiful smile of hers, past the tubes that violated her. She motioned for water, but she was only given a damp cloth to put on her parched lips.

"Banny, what have we done to you?" I asked myself. I loved this wonderful and beautiful woman. She was like a mother to me. Had we inadvertently done her a great injustice?

I don't know exactly where the answer lies. Perhaps more knowledge and understanding should be given the public in regard to this life-support matter. Maybe it is not the thing to do to a person who is 80 and whose condition was so critical.

Would Banny have been better off in a Hospice program where she could have been with her children and grandchildren? She could have told us what was so very much on her mind in a more dignified setting for death.

The nurses told us Banny knew everything that was going on. Most of the time this was not a blessing. But when we told her we loved her and she moved her lips to reply, this helped.

OUR THREE CHILDREN stayed in touch by telephone. When Banny's condition worsened, Barry, the eldest, decided he was flying out as soon as he could get a plane.

"I don't want to get there for her funeral," he said. "I want to see her while she is still alive." All three of our children loved Banny. They never had to wonder how she felt about them. "When she looks at me," Barry said, "she looks like she could just eat me up. There is a special look she gives. No one else looks that way."

Barry arrived at the hospital Wednesday afternoon, October 12. Banny had died that morning. He didn't have a chance to see her and to tell her his special feelings. That night he went for a long walk. He is a private person and he grieves in private.

The funeral was Friday and Steve and Eleanor flew in from Chattanooga and Memphis respectively. They were also devastated by the death of their beloved grandmother.

During the funeral service, Banny was described as "a woman

of great wisdom and great love." Her love for her family was equated with wisdom. Those who knew Banny agreed with this summation of a life filled with unselfish love.

AFTER BANNY WAS LAID TO REST, we were still in a state of shock. We had driven to Florida, hoping we would stay with Banny until she was well enough to come back to her apartment. We would then try to get some nice lady to stay with her and help take care of her until she got well enough to come back to Chattanooga and be with her family.

However, it didn't work out that way. We arrived in time to talk with her a couple of days. Then followed those agonizing days of suffering for her. After her mother was put on the life-support system, Betty, who is not too tall, would stand on a stool and lean over and kiss her and tell her, "I love you, Mama."

She bravely tried to hold back tears so Banny wouldn't see. We took turns trying to be brave. Banny was the brave one as she tried to reassure us with a smile and a squeeze of the hand. She had worried about us not getting enough rest and whether we had eaten.

When we saw she was continually "slipping" despite the tubes and oxygen, and watched her painfully gasping for each breath, we asked the doctor if she could be spared more of the ordeal she was going through. We were told this could not "legally be done." Earlier, we had been told otherwise. "This can be reversed," we had been assured.

At this point we wondered if science and technology had outdistanced ethics and humaneness in a mad race in the field of medicine. And then we are reminded of people who have been subjected to this ultimate system for staying alive and have lived to say they are glad to be here.

It is not an easy question to answer. It weighs heavily on those who make the decision. Those for whom the decision is made are defenseless.

AFTER BANNY DIED, Betty remained the courageous little trouper. She put on a brave front in the presence of company. At night when we were alone she'd break down and cry for her mama.

"I feel like an orphan," she said. "Now I know exactly what you meant when you said you felt like an orphan after your father and mother died."

Being grown doesn't keep you from feeling this way. That unique love cannot be replaced. No one ever will look at you in that special way.

During these bad times our children came to our support. Friends have offered their condolences. Flowers and cards have poured in. We are grateful. It helps.

If one lives long enough, bad times will come around. But these serve to emphasize the preciousness and precariousness of life. It is to be lived, and loving is an essential part of living.

I dedicate this column to Banny. The kids began calling her "Banny" and the name remained. It fitted. She was one of the sweetest ladies who ever lived. Ask her nurses, Kim and MaryAnn, who marveled at her uncomplaining bravery.

I didn't mean to burden you, but Banny was uppermost in my mind. I wanted to share a celebration of a life with you. There was no room in Banny's heart for pettiness and meanness, only love. And that she gave fully and unstintingly. We all learned from her. Perhaps we also learned from her ordeal.

We miss you Banny. There'll never be anyone else like you!

Just wish you had come back home to us . . . earlier.

TEACHERS: SOME EXCELLED, OTHERS FLUNKED

I WASN'T ONE OF THOSE GENIUSES who couldn't get enough of school. There were times when I thought it would be dangerous to overload a young brain with too much knowledge.

Besides, what good would it do me to learn to diagram sentences and to work algebra problems? Most people I knew had jobs that didn't require heavy doses of these subjects.

But some good teachers were able to answer these and other questions. They did it by encouraging and by going over and over their subjects. I once thought teachers got extra pay for keeping students after class for more instruction. Why else would they go to this trouble?

I learned it wasn't the extra pay — which they didn't and still don't get — but the extra interest in their pupils.

"There is no reason in the world why you can't learn this," said such a teacher. "You've just got to concentrate more on what you're doing." And when that magic moment arrived and the student saw the light, not one, but two people were beaming like beacons.

One such teacher helped make sense out of arithmetic and mathematics for students who didn't have a natural penchant for figures. She set up a buying and selling situation with customers and salespeople and play money. Suddenly it dawned on youngsters that their parents used math in their everyday life.

It was a fun and practical way to learn, and it worked.

LIFE IS NOT A BED of roses and the thorns appeared in the person of my fifth-grade teacher. She was not just tough, she was downright mean and took an almost sadistic delight in frightening those in her class.

I later found out I was not the only one whose good grades plummeted under the tirades of this tyrant. She literally petrified us with her high-pitched scoldings.

It wouldn't have made me feel much better about myself to know she was suffering from a thyroid condition. Whatever the cause, it was taking its toll on me and other classmates.

My parents wondered what was happening, but it never occurred to us innocents to ever blame anything on a teacher. That would have been mutinous, and besides it wouldn't have gone over with my parents. A teacher occupied a high position, and she was almost sacrosanct.

I learned then how someone can take advantage of his or her position and ride roughshod over those who are helpless to defend themselves.

The next year I learned about compassion from my sixth grade teacher. Mrs. Blevins was a beautiful person in the finest sense of the word.

She immediately recognized a student whose psyche had been scarred. Her daughter had taught the same student and had given him "A's." Other teachers had also thought he was a good student. So why the falling of grades?

Apparently Mrs. Blevins had seen this happen before with students in the fifth grade. She knew what was going on and immediately started taking steps to repair the damage. She began rebuilding my confidence.

That year she made certain I had the lead in a play. It wasn't my acting ability that got me the part. I now understand she was trying to put my shattered Humpty Dumpty ego back together again.

Bless you Mrs. Blevins, I will never forget you. Not only did I again enjoy going to school, but you also taught me the importance of compassion and trying to help others pick up the pieces.

JUST HOW PROFICIENT another teacher was in teaching third-grade material, I don't recall. But I remember this teacher because of her blatant insensitivity.

She was telling us about the importance of proper diet and decided that a chubby youngster was the example of a kid who drank milk. He sat in front of the class with a "milk drinker" sign. Back then, being on the heavier side was considered a sign of good health.

To illustrate the "coffee drinker," she selected a skinny student from the other side of the tracks. He sat in front of the class with a coffee sign. He was known to be from a very poor family and his clean but shoddy clothes were proof positive.

The teacher had on other occasions commented on the way he was dressed, apparently not worrying about his feelings nor the poverty in his home. A statement such as, "Where in the world did you get that outfit?" could ensure gales of laughter from the students as he squirmed and looked down at the floor.

Even a youngster could see the prejudice and lack of feelings. At the time I wondered why an adult, especially a teacher, couldn't understand the embarrassment she was causing this little guy.

I can still see him trying to smile bravely behind his "coffee drinker" sign.

I hope he turned out to be a fine, substantial citizen despite the buzz saw type of treatment he received from this elementary school teacher. If he did do well, it wasn't because of her.

"OLD LADY SMITH," who must have been at least into her senile twenties, was one heck of a teacher. We've all been lucky to have had such a teacher.

I remember her giving me an unusually good grade on a math test. This was not the rule for me. I was very proud of the grade but noticed she had taken off five points because of a misspelled word.

Already flushed with my rare math victory, I protested: "But that isn't fair. This is a math test, not a spelling test."

This fine teacher said something to the effect that: "Spelling and writing are important, whether it's on a math test paper or in writing a letter."

It turned out she was right, of course, about spelling and the choice of the right words. It helps in any occupation.

THERE IS HARDLY a reader who doesn't remember at least one or two great teachers who taught him more than just subject matter.

They made a vital difference in young lives and their pupils will never forget them. They were important not only in teaching us subjects but in shaping our attitudes and character.

GETTING RID OF
JUNK AND MEMORIES

MY WIFE IS ECSTATIC because I am finally doing something about "our messy garage."

For years she has urged me to clean it out because it has become a catchall for anything I want to save. And for years I've been putting off this job because it's hard for a "saver" to throw anything away when he likes to save almost everything.

I believe each home should have at least one big room for the storehousing of items that may come in handy — and even more importantly for the tangible preservation of memories.

On one of the recent occasions when her patience was wearing precariously thin, my frustrated wife took me by the hand and together we went downstairs for still another look at the "garage."

The large area was originally built for storing an auto or two, but it has never been used for such a purpose. That's what the carport is for. To me it was a singular blessing to have the extra space for things I needed to save.

"You mean like these tires?" my wife asked.

"Why not? You never know when they'll come in handy."

"But if they weren't worn thin you wouldn't have taken them off in the first place," my wife reasoned.

I don't like it when she checkmates me with such irrefutable logic.

"So why do you keep those beat-up old tires?" she pressed on.

"Just because," I said, realizing the explanation sounded juvenile. So I had to strengthen my case by admitting:

"Those old tires remind me of our cars we once drove." The second I said that I realized I had made a tactical blunder.

"I don't believe you said that," said my wife. "You can't save everything in the world because it reminds you of something."

She pointed to the old suitcases, piles of newspapers and magazines, books, pictures, barbells, cable stretchers, old gym clothes, handball gloves, jars full of nails and screws, mementos of vacation trips and political conventions, playbills, receipts of long-since paid bills and many other items I considered worth saving.

She also noted tangled garden hoses, lawn mowers that didn't work and one that did, a weed cutter, a broken stationary bike, cans half full of oxidized, non-usable paint, garden tools and seeders I hadn't used in over a decade. And then there was stuff I'll have to admit was just plain junk.

"I'm embarrassed when anyone sees this place," said my wife. I reminded her male visitors invariably say, "This doesn't look as bad as my garage."

"They're just trying to be nice," said my wife. "They're not going to say this place looks like a junkyard, which it does. Please do something about this," pleaded my wife who is one of the neatest people I know. I sometimes refer to her as Mrs. Clean. "Let me get someone to clean up this mess," she urged.

"But how will he know what and what not to throw away?" I asked. "There are tons of memories down here, and I don't have the heart to just get rid of them without a thought. Who knows what I've got in these nine or 10 old suitcases. For instance, here are my army discharge papers. I bet there are letters in there written during the war."

"Then let me get you help," she urged. "You've forgotten what's in most of those old suitcases. You wouldn't even miss it."

She gingerly touched one of the dust-covered treasure chests. "Look," she said, "the letters are yellow and have been dripped on by a leak from the pipes over the years."

She insisted "most of that stuff is so damaged it won't be of any use to you or anyone else."

I reminded her the years have also eroded me physically and have left their mark on my once passable physiognomy but that I'm still of some use.

"That's different," she said with her blue-eyed smile that always could get me to do her bidding, although in this case it took almost 30 years to start the "garage" cleanup job.

Women are supposed to have a goodly share of sentimentality, understanding and emotion, but I believe this is more than balanced out by their practicality.

My memories were piling up and something had to go. Besides, Betty had shown an enormous amount of patience and restraint. She had suggested I even clean out the garage on the installment plan, a little at a time, moldy suitcase by suitcase.

"But first, please get rid of those tires. I can't even find enough floor to sweep, and I hardly have enough room for the garbage cans."

Garbage is a big item with us.

THE YOUNG MAN helping clean out the garage sensed my reluctance to part with the newspapers and magazines and letters. The suitcases were dusted off and stacked in orderly fashion. I'll examine those contents real soon. I probably have

some column material there. Also saved were books of all variet-
ies, including those used in school by our children.

They may want to keep those books and school uniforms and
show them to their children, but I doubt it. After youngsters cut
apron strings, they also cut most ties with the past. People are
more sentimental as they become older. Time has more meaning for them.

The young man was careful as he threw away the newspapers
and magazines. In between the pages were more long-forgotten
pictures.

The magazines over the years had amounted to a huge stack.
If I had the room, I'd keep every one. They remind me of time's
passage and they're probably collector's items. But, what the
heck, throw them out.

"Wow," said the young man, "this magazine was published in
1965. That was a long time before I was born."

In that year I was already a middle-aged husband and newsman,
with the joys and worries that go along with being a family man.

My young worker picked up on my mood and concern and
every now and then would double check with me:

"Is this OK to throw away?"

"Yeah," I replied, "its OK." But it really wasn't.

It's never OK to throw away memories — especially the good
ones.

REGRETS THAT CAN PULL YOU DOWN

THERE ARE regrets and there are REGRETS.

Some you can build on and learn from. These are the bricks which at the outset were not properly used but can be put back with the stronger, longer-lasting mortar of experience.

Other regrets are useless material. They have no value and will not add to the structure of your life. And if you are determined to carry them around with you, they will only serve to weigh you down.

A case in point: When I was covering the courthouse and politics as a somewhat younger newsman, I was acquainted with an older attorney who carried with him the heavy load of regret of once having made a definitive "stupid decision." It had eaten on him ever since.

A fine lawyer, who won more than his share of cases, he would have been highly insulted if anyone even insinuated he lacked judgment. If you had called him stupid, you would have had a fight on your hands.

And yet, at least once a year, this talented, highly successful attorney would stop me in the halls or in an office to recount the "stupid" mistake he had made many years before. He was so caught up with this particular regret, he forgot he had already told me about it, numerous times.

It was as if he felt compelled to recite this litany. Although it was painful for him to give me the details, he would do so. Mercifully for both of us, it was brief.

"I COULD KICK MYSELF for the stupid decision I made back then," he would say. (Back then was when a little-known soft drink called Coca-Cola was first being bottled. At the time it was one of many struggling soft drinks on the market. Most of the others literally went down the drain of competition.)

"Do you know what I did?"

I knew what he had done. He had told me about it many times during the years. It was a festering regret. One he wouldn't or couldn't turn loose.

"I had done some work for an important client, and it came to about $5,000 in legal fees. That was big money back in those days. Well, this gentleman asked me to come by his office to discuss the fees. It wasn't that he was dissatisfied. He said he had a deal he was willing to make.

"The deal was that either I take a check for the $5,000 fee or be paid with twice that amount, $10,000, in Coca-Cola stock. I don't think I thought about that deal more than a few seconds, and I told him I'd rather have the $5,000, which I could be sure of. The soft drink stock was a gamble. Coca-Cola didn't mean any more to me than Quacky Duck or any other brand. So I took the $5,000. What a jerk."

I understood what was eating on him, but I reminded him that was one bridge he should burn. "Besides, how were you to know that Coca-Cola was going to make it so big? Almost anyone with good business judgment would have done the same thing you did."

The attorney apparently was so busy kicking himself for his "stupid" blunder, he hardly heard what I said.

"Do you realize that by now that $10,000 in Coca-Cola stock would have made me a multimillionaire?"

And then he recalled how many times that success-destined stock has split in recent years and how the value had soared and how on today's market the money would have compounded and quadrupled.

He probably has worn out several adding machines going over these problematical geometric gymnastics, which have left his spirit tired, dragging and aching.

I haven't seen him in several years. Hopefully, he has found peace with himself on this money-absorbed earth or he is where money or soft drinks don't matter.

ONE OF THE MOST useless regrets we have heard of was not from a fellow who missed out on making a nice chunk of money, but . . . let me tell you about him:

He owned a water-logged tract of land in what, at the time, was an unproductive area of the county. He had bought the land in what was a hardship sale and by his own admission, he paid "very little for it."

For years he had wondered if he had made a good investment, even at the relatively small sum he had paid for the large tract. Nothing seemed to be happening in that part of the county. For years there was very little action. And then, as with business ventures and building, things started moving.

"That area became a hot item, and I began getting offers. I think I paid about $6,000 for the land, and I figured I had held on to it for so long and had paid taxes on it for so long that I ought to at least triple my money."

The offers continued, and he wisely held out for a length of time. "But when it got up to $100,000, I decided I'd turn it loose. The fellow who made the offer said he was buying the land for speculative purposes. He said he might have to keep it for 10 or more years before he could sell it at a reasonable profit, but he was willing to take his chances."

The deal was made and for about two years the businessman was happy about his profit.

I RECALL HEARING FROM him on many occasions prior to the $100,000 sale that he must have been "out to lunch" when he bought the land. "It stays under water half the time."

So when he got the $100,000 offer, he jumped at it. He unloaded that water-soaked property. Quite a profit from a $6,000 investment. "Beats municipal bonds," he gloated.

He was a happy man until, almost two years to the day he sold it, the purchaser of his land in turn sold it to a corporation for $200,000.

"He doubled what he had paid me."

"So?"

"So? Look how much I could have made on that land if I'd had sense enough to hold on to it for another two years?"

But how would he know that the price would sky-rocket like that?

"Well, apparently the guy who bought the land from me must have known something. Why else would he have paid me $100,000 for land that was covered with water half of the year?"

He said something else about the purchaser of his land that wasn't very complimentary to the purchaser's family tree and implied the dirty so-and-so had tricked if not crooked him.

"He probably had heard about that company and knew it was going to build at the time he bought it."

"So what?" I reiterated. "So what?" he repeated. "How would you like to lose $100,000 just like that?" He didn't ask me how I'd like to pick up $100,000 on something I paid $6,000 for. A nice return, indeed.

I told him he worried too much about what happened to the property after it was out of his hands instead of remembering the profit he had made. "By now, the land alone is probably worth a million," I added.

I shouldn't have said that. It will probably give him even more cause for regret. I wouldn't want to be responsible for anything bad happening to him.

He's already worried enough about that $100,000 he did NOT make.

A MIRACLE IS REPEATED

AFTER MONTHS OF ANTICIPATION — nine to be exact — the exciting event finally took place.

The main attraction was a healthy, beautiful baby boy. He and his mother are both fine.

The father is doing all right and his feet are now starting to touch the ground again. He has had three weeks to get used to the idea of being a father, but the marvel of it all still boggles his mind.

We remembered the feeling with our own firstborn. It's as if this miracle had never happened to anyone else. This was brought back to us when we stood with the proud father outside the observation room filled with these tiny human beings.

Some were sleeping. Some were crying and squirming. All were new arrivals on this earth. Hopefully, most of them were welcome and would be loved, protected and cherished by their parents.

"There he is," said the beaming father. "That real handsome guy over there. That chesty one."

It was out of character for this young man to brag about anything. He is usually low-keyed and reserved. But here he was not only showing animation but great pride in the fact that his and his wife's son was starting off in life with fine looks and a manly physique.

We stared and grinned at that boy baby. It was a very special moment.

A nurse, who noticed our more than casual interest in this new arrival, picked him up and brought him closer to us so we could really good a good peek.

We must have looked like two grinning idiots as we pondered whom the baby resembled. Anyone who has played this game knows there are no solid clues. Everyone has his own ides as to whom "the baby favors."

This is all academic, because the baby's looks will change time and again as the years go by.

The nurse put the baby boy back in his blue-blanketed crib.

THE PROUD FATHER SAID: "I still can't believe it. I still can't believe that little guy there is my very own son." He smiled and shook his head as he tried to take it all in.

We didn't ask him what was running through his mind. We didn't have to. The same thing had happened to the fellow at his side.

The circumstances were different. He didn't get to see his firstborn — also a son — until he got back from overseas during World War II.

But the sense of marvel was the same at the endless renewal and continuity of life. Indeed, it was as if this miracle of birth had never before happened to a man and wife.

And then came the overwhelming sense of responsibility for the health, welfare and future of this little human being who was utterly dependent on his mother and father.

Unlike many other living creatures, he would be relatively

helpless and unable to protect himself for years to come.

There is something inherently appealing and basic about being protector and provider for another human being, especially one who is your very own.

The full circle is complete. You now understand the joys and apprehensions of your own parents. Maybe they were — in their own fumbling way — looking out for your best interests along with the selfish satisfaction of wanting a child they would "be proud of."

These and other thoughts ran through my mind as I looked at a paticularly handsome baby boy in that room full of crying, sleeping and squirming newly arrived humanity.

"What do you think about him, Dad?" my son asked in rhetorical fashion. "Isn't he beautiful, just like I told you?"

Adam Shayne is our first grandson.

Hang on folks! Life gets more interesting and "beautiful" as it goes along.

EACH GENERATION GOES through the same doubts, guilt and confusion in regard to the "proper way" to bring up a family. There is the concern about being too heavy handed or too permissive.

In our own case, with each succeeding child we eased up just a little bit. Our first son experienced a carryover of the First Sergeant School of Child Rearing. With his own son, we see a chance for him to take the middle-of-the-road approach.

"The main thing is for him to know that you and LeNet love him," we told our son. "If he knows that, he will better understand what you are trying to do when you discipline him."

And then almost to my surprise, I heard my grandfatherly advice: "Try to have as much fun with him as you can. It'll make life more enjoyable for the entire family.

"Sure, you'll make some mistakes. We all do. But don't carry a lot of guilt feelings around for the mistakes you do make. Just do the best you can, and it'll all work out."

The new father put his arm around my shoulder.

"Dad," he said, "thanks for the advice. I know what you mean. You and Mom must not have made too many mistakes. You meant well . . . and I love you."

That assuaged some of the "heavy-handed" guilt I've carried over the years in regard to our first son's upbringing. Our daughter and our second son had coped with less stern treatment as the "old man" had mellowed. We had more "fun" with our younger son.

Taking a cue from the middle-of-the-road, "don't be too tough" advice we gave Barry in regard to our new grandson, he said just before we left:

"Now you wouldn't spoil old Adam, would you?

"We'll see," I said as I returned a proud smile of my own.

A Survey Reminds Us
We Forget

We ARE BEMUSED AT LEAST once a week by surveys which arrive at the obvious. Would you believe, for example, that students whose parents help them with their homework make better grades than those whose parents don't seem to care?

Another study showed that children raised by two parents had fewer emotional, social and school problems than those in one-parent families or with no parents at all.

Now comes the latest in the list of scientific studies. This one shows that children's feelings and their psyches are more easily hurt and bruised than adults realize. Being embarrassed and humiliated were seen as principal causes for concern among children as well as being thought of as bad.

But this survey is apparently not as obvious as the other ones. We, as adults, seem to have forgotten what this study reminds us of, and if it helps make life just a little easier for some of the small fry in a tough old world, it will have been worthwhile.

Judging by our own experiences and those of other parents, most of us can stand some reminding about the feelings and emotions of those who have been entrusted to us.

A parent who wouldn't think of idly standing by as his child was being harmed, might unwittingly allow his child to be emotionally harmed because he or she has forgotten how it feels to be a child.

Parents also forget that those little guys and girls are not just small adults, but formative, spongelike, sensitive little people with big questions about life and fears that are magnified many times because of lack of experience and reference points and the inability to take action.

Try to remember how it was when you were growing up in a world full of "no-nos" and very few explanations for them. Remember how difficult it was for you to feel like a unique individual with proper self-esteem when you were constantly being treated like a second-class citizen whose every move was dictated or criticized by parents or teachers.

And then think how your fragile self-esteem could be shattered by some ill-chosen words or actions. Then try to remember why the opinions of others — including your peers — are so important to young people.

They haven't had a chance to make their own track record. They haven't proven to themselves who they are and the stuff they are made of. So outside approval is especially important to them.

Then consider the importance of approval in your own life, even now, and you will perhaps recall the awful, ostracized feeling of a youngster who doesn't feel he belongs in school or in games. And then remember if he is starved for even a minimum amount of approval at home, he or she will double the efforts to find acceptance among peers, even if it is from the wrong crowd.

One's ego, young or old, needs to be constantly nourished. During the formative years, it is an extremely fragile thing.

I'VE OFTEN WONDERED if I had the opportunity of doing the parent bit over again, would I have been such a stickler for discipline. This is one of those questions that arises from hindsight, and I would like to think I would take a somewhat gentler approach. Conditioning leaves its mark, however, and I probably couldn't allow a child of mine to get too out of hand. My parents seldom allowed this and corrected accordingly.

But perhaps more patience and sense of humor and more tolerance for the antics of these little inexperienced explorers would result in happier days and less friction and tears for everyone, parents included.

Parents are in the position of literally flying by the seat of their pants. Even the advice given by so-called experts varies widely with some advocating mild punishment and others going to the extreme of "reasoning it out" with young charges who have not fully developed their reasoning powers.

So, that gets us back to square one in which you are asked to try and remember how you felt as children — what you liked and what frightened you. I remember liking the approval of my parents and my teachers. What frightened me was not getting that approval, especially from my parents.

During my childhood, an adult represented authority, whether that adult was a parent, a teacher or a neighbor. If you were braced by a teacher or neighbor for stepping over the line or not toeing the mark, the odds were great you wouldn't tell your parents about your problem. Likely as not, one authority figure would agree with the other and that would be to your disadvantage if you were a youngster back then.

MOST PARENTS WANT TO GIVE their children everything they feel is important for their present and future happiness. A parent wants his children to have more than he had in creature comforts and in education.

That's why I'm reminded by the latest survey that it is important for children to have a healthy amount of self-esteem and pride. This ranks right up there with the other fine things we wish for our young. Parents of previous generations did not overly ponder this question. Theirs was a simpler approach: You behave or else.

Discipline is necessary to conform to certain standards of society. But, in retrospect, it seems discipline should not be so heavy handed that pride and self-esteem are bruised, with resultant damage to the ego.

And therein lies a dilemma. In a world universally known for its toughness, cynicism and danger, where is the balance between bringing up an individual too soft for his or her own good or too tough for his or her personal happiness and relationships with others?

You don't want to raise a namby-pamby or a bully. There should be a happy medium.

If the survey didn't do anything but remind us that children are ever-changing, ever-learning little people with their own sensitivities and problems that loom bigger than life, it would have served a purpose. Maybe one less parent or teacher will tell a child he or she is stupid or bad and have that child believe the higher authority of an adult who is seemingly always right.

I can still remember the impact of a lady customer's kind words when she told my father she liked for this 10-year-old to "wait" on her at my parents' grocery. Prior to the days of the supermarkets, every item had to be taken from shelf or counter by the clerk.

She gave me a big smile as she bragged on me. I can still see her face and feel the warmth of her words that reassured a youngster in an adult working world. I thought that love must feel the way I felt toward this lovely lady.

GETTING ON A
'HIGH' WITH THE BOYS

IT MADE ME WONDER which world is the real world.

This occurred after the almost annual pilgrimage to the Smokies that I take with our two sons after they've convinced me there is life away from the newspaper.

We've been taking these hiking trips for many years and each one has been different. What remains constant is the excitement and pleasure of the trip and the renewed acquaintance of father and sons. The change of scenery and pace is conducive to great conversations and insightful exchanges of ideas and views on life in general.

Each time I'm impressed with the analytical and philosophical tone of our sons' remarks, since they too are also practical enough to give their demanding jobs the time and effort required. Yet, as we ride toward our motel this side of Knoxville, there are numerous aesthetic subjects discussed that are seldom touched on at home.

Heretofore, Barry, Steve and I have always made the trip in one car. And we stay in one large motel room with two double beds and a rollaway bed. The fun begins at the outset of the trip, and then it picks up in tempo. The relaxation is felt from the time we head out. The boys drive. I just sit back and grin.

But this time Steve's job required him to leave Saturday

instead of Friday, the day Barry and I left. He was to meet us at the motel Saturday afternoon after we got back from our hike in the Smokies.

Friday night we dined at the motel and looked forward to the arrival of the third party. We have always stopped at this motel. It has become a tradition and since the food, lodging and service are great, why not? Also great was the conversation between son and father.

SATURDAY, WE GOT UP early, had a hearty breakfast and headed for the mountains. We drove through several tinsel towns with "something to do for everyone," especially kids, and then without warning, almost burst upon the kind of attraction that only Mother Nature can offer. The contrast between the man-made and natural scenery was almost a shock and was a reminder of nature's grandeur and man's puny effort to upstage her.

Barry, who is an avid hiker, camper and nature lover, pointed out various vegetation, trees and rock formations, some which were millions of years old. Icy-cold streams gurgled over rocks, attracting fishermen and other outdoor enthusiasts. Pink dog-woods dotted the moss and tree-studded forest and every turn of the road presented another view of the breathtaking panorama.

"Makes you wonder why other things seemed so important yesterday," observed Barry.

And the higher the elevation, the more one felt a return to the winter left behind several months ago or the one that is on nature's calendar schedule a few months down the road. Little by little the vegetation changed and then there it was: Snow, piled in drifts up to several feet and spread like a white blanket over the bosom of the earth.

"Let's get out and take a look," said my son. This also meant

let's take in more of the heady, unadulterated air on this cloud-
less, pristine day that was perfect to relieve one of job cares and
other concerns.

What it also meant was Barry had spotted a likely hiking path
and was eager to hit the trail. I would have been more eager, but
the mountain air was cold although the sun shone with a brilliance
seldom seen in busy, cloud-shrouded cities.

ONE THING I'VE NOTICED about the hikes we take; they
aren't as long or as vigorous as they were a few years ago. As a
rusting ex-athlete who tries to stay in reasonable shape, this
bothers me. Could this old boy, meaning me, be slowing down?
I know I had been riding for a while and that one gets a little
stoved up and stiff from sitting that long, but wasn't it taking me
a little longer to get out of the car this time than last time and the
time before?

Barry assured me it was the combination of the length of the
trip and the coolness of the mountain air that made me squeak
and grunt as I tried to unwind and stand up.

Once I got my engine going, Barry pointed to a hiking path in
a by-the-way fashion as if not to intimidate me. The path was
dampish but comparatively smooth. It went over a bridge which
looked down on water rushing over ancient rocks.

"I'll bet that water is freezing," I thought. I wasn't exactly hot
for the idea of taking a long hike. It was too darn cold, but I
didn't say so.

I looked at the massive stones in the stream and wondered
how long they had been there and how much longer they would
be here than subsequent generations of city mountaineers. They
didn't speak or think, but they survived.

Barry had already hit the trail, albeit at a very moderate pace
more suitable for those whose engines required longer warming-

up periods. I followed and found the walking fun except for my creaking legs and the steam from my radiator. The temperature just wasn't right and I wasn't going to press my luck. I'm afraid I didn't let Barry even stretch out before I decided to walk back to the car. "That's okay," Barry said. "It's too cold to hike much today."

Did he say too "cold" or too "old," I thought. Getting back in the car was easier than getting out. It seemed most of my vigorous "action" was getting in and out of the car. Times have changed.

BEFORE WE HEADED BACK, we drove to higher elevation and more snow. We stopped for a few moments at an out-of-the-way camping site where families had set up tents and were cooking out of doors. We opened a window in order to poach on the aroma of the succulent morsels.

We drove as far as we could to higher elevation, but the snow and ice had blocked off the road to Clingman's Dome. I was also thwarted in an effort to make a snowball. The snow was a hunk of solid ice.

We drove down the circuitous road and watched the vegetation change and the snow disappear. We had entered another calendar zone and pink dogwoods again dotted the beautiful mountainscape.

Again we left the awesomeness of nature and entered man's tinsel, gaudy and pitiful imitation of nature's beauty and excitement.

Soon we were back in the familiar welcoming confines of our motel. I rested up a little from the "hike," and Barry did some reading in the courtyard. No newspapers or TV news.

Then the eagerly awaited third party arrived and the fun again accelerated. The conversation never lagged. There seemed to

be endless subjects to explore and things to laugh about, including ourselves. We again dined in the familiar motel dining room
and the conversation and fun continued until we finally retired
for the night.

WE WERE EARLY RISERS Sunday morning. Barry had to go
to his office, and Steve would drive me home where our daughter, Eleanor, was visiting. Again the conversation was great, and
we came close to solving a few of the world's problems.

The trip was too short. Then it was home, and sister and
mother greeted the younger brother. Monday was the other day
I was taking off. But I had already noticed an abrupt change. I
wanted to meet Betty for lunch and this required me to eye the
clock so I would be on time. And there were several things I
needed to do.

Clocks had little meaning on the mountain trip. But now I was
already getting a taste of deadline.

I watched television and saw scene after scene of murderous
violence by hijackers, violence in the Middle East, explosion of
an army depot in Pakistan which may have killed thousands,
computer hackers who could wipe out most of the world's
information, Los Angeles crackdown on drug-dealing and murderous gangs, huge Texas drug seizures, Senate hearing on
organized crime in America and the touting of "Fatal Attraction"
for Oscar honors.

This, along with "dangerous" cucumbers that had been sprayed
with deadly pesticides, was seen at one sitting on Monday, the
day before I returned to work.

The veneer on my newly-acquired relaxed attitude was wearing
thin. I was beginning to feel uptight enough and high-strung
enough to get back in gear and return to work.

I had come back to the real world. Or had I?

I'm Gonna Sit Right Down
And . . .

WHEN WAS THE LAST TIME you answered a letter or card on the same day you received it? If you said, "recently," that would be most unusual. If you said, "I always do," then you are a rare bird.

If your answer is "I can't recall" or "never," you are eligible to join the millions who put off answering mail.

I don't know what there is about not immediately answering a letter or note, but it is a bad habit that plagues most of us, or so it seems.

I've tried to analyze my reasons for not answering mail the same day I receive it. I'll admit up front it sounds sort of flimsy, as if I'm rationalizing. But here goes:

If a letter about a column is kind and thoughtful, I find myself reading the letter over at least a couple of times. Depending on the contents of the letter and the kind of a day it has been, I may even give it three or four readings as I bask in the warmth and good will of the letter writer. Such kind letters act as a comfort blanket to help fend off frustration and bruised ego.

So if I feel that way about the letters and toward the readers who wrote them, I'm surely going to give more than casual thought to how I answer them. After all, if a reader takes the time and effort plus the cost of a stamp to communicate his feelings, he deserves to have more than a cursory reply.

Some time ago a form letter had been suggested as a time-saving device, but after noting the cold and impersonal way it sounded, I opted to sit down and write out my answers, usually in longhand. Besides, some letters are more personal, thought-provoking and open than others, and they deserve more thought and effort.

But what gets me and my fellow procrastinators in trouble is that once you put off answering a letter, and several more arrive, you are compounding the situation. And there is a point you finally reach where you are almost too embarrassed to answer. You have put off answering too long, and you feel like an ingrate for doing so. That unanswered letter may have made your day, and now it is weighing on your conscience.

I should answer some letters I received today, but that doesn't seem fair since I've got several already waiting in line to be answered. They were here first.

THEN THERE ARE the letters you automatically put off answering, but for different reasons. These are negative letters that have nothing uplifting about them. They weren't written with the thought of making your day. They guarantee the opposite.

I learned long ago to put off answering such letters. Never, but never, reply to a letter when you are not in a tolerant, understanding mood. Once you've committed your thoughts and feelings to paper, they are here and can be thrown squarely back at you.

So, you put these aside until you can think of a reasonable, if not clever, answer. Invariably these letters seem to require more thought than the other kind because you are on thinner ice and not in as friendly territory.

And when you've waited longer than you should to answer this type of letter, there isn't the guilt feeling attached to the complimentary kind.

HERE IS ANOTHER PITFALL of putting it off: Letters can be lost and addresses misplaced and this causes more concern. And even worse things can happen during these too long intervals between the letter or phone call and the response.

A friend of my father's had always had a very hearty and sincere greeting for me ever since I was old enough to walk downtown by myself and past his clothing store. You've heard the expression of two people "hitting it off." Well, that was the way I felt about Mr. Abe and the way he felt about me.

I may have been in a young hurry, but I'd better not be in too big a hurry to chat with the old boy. He was a big, sturdy man with a vise-like handshake, and he took great pleasure that I was getting bigger and stronger as the months went by.

"Let's shake hands. Let's see what you've got," he'd say. "Not bad, not bad."

And Mr. Abe would question me about my school, and as the years went by he'd ask me about my social life and grin at me and sometimes grab me around the neck in a wrestling hold.

He had two grown sons who worked with him in the store, but he apparently had plenty of room in his big heart to temporarily adopt this skinny kid who amused him with the latest corny joke he'd heard at school that day.

He also thought highly of my father, and he'd tell me so and this didn't hurt the way I felt about this jolly, fatherly business-man. He always seemed to have time to talk and joke with a kid who in those days didn't get too much of that kind of adult attention unless there was something very wrong or exceptionally right.

OUR FRIENDSHIP continued for years, but the years finally took their toll and Mr. Abe retired and we lost track of each other until I got a phone call from him at the newspaper. I immediately recognized his voice although it lacked the resonant tone and timbre of the voice I remembered in my youth.

It was Mr. Abe and he personalized his call by referring to me as "you rascal" and how's the "big boy"? These were two of his favorite appellations in referring to me.

"I'm fine, Mr. Abe, and how are you?"

"I'm getting older," he said. "I'll bet you can out-handshake me now."

I told him, "I doubt it," remembering that once bone-crunching handshake of his.

He said he was in reasonably good health, but the reason he was calling was to tell me he now resided at Alexian Village and he would like for me to come visit him.

Of course I promised and meant it and told him I enjoyed our conversation very much. I also got very busy as soon as I hung up and put the conversation on the back burner until a few months later when I got a letter from Mr. Abe. He again extended an invitation to me to come and see him "and let's talk about the old times, and maybe we can laugh the way we used to."

He said he was well cared for but he got lonesome for people he knew in his more active days and that if "you can find time to spend at least an hour with me for old time's sake, it will be a real pleasure for me and I'd appreciate it."

He confided that his own children were also very busy and couldn't see him as often as he liked but he understood "that is the way of the world . . . The older generation steps down and the next generation has the responsibilities of making a living for their family . . . I know that's the way it is and I know you also are a very busy man, big boy.

"I just want to remind you about my phone call and also to

remind you I'm not getting younger, although I think I am better looking now than I ever was. Ha ha."

I got the letter at the beginning of a week. This time I was going to see my old friend and talk about those more vigorous days. I started to answer the letter, but then I reasoned I would see Mr. Abe that week. And then it was next week for sure. I told my wife I was going.

That was the week I saw Mr. Abe's obituary in the paper. He didn't get my letter or a visit. I read the obituary several times. It seemed so cold and impersonal for my old friend who enjoyed life so much.

I wrote a few more lines in the obituary. It was self-serving and didn't ease me very much.

I wish I had written a reply to his letter. Better still, I wish I had taken the time to see him for "old time's sake."

ALL HEROES ARE NOT ON THE BATTLEFIELD

THIS PAST APRIL OUR DAUGHTER, ELEANOR, got a medical report that shook her up and maybe alarmed us even more. Since then she has taken the necessary steps to get back to her normally fine health.

She has gone about the business of getting well with a minimum of self-pity or anger.

She's a fighter. In fact on numerous occasions she has had to remind her dad: "Please don't look so sad. It makes me feel bad when I see you so down. I'll get well but you need to help me be upbeat and optimistic."

I'd try not to show my concern, but she'd see me slip every now and then and I had to start watching myself. Her mother also agreed being positive was very important in Eleanor's recovery.

Of course they are both right, but you know how it is with fathers and daughters, especially when she is the only daughter. "But this is nothing new," said her mother. "You've always spoiled her."

Could be. But this time for a very good reason. And besides, I've admired how she has bitten the bullet and been a good sport about it. First, there was chemotherapy once every three weeks for 18 weeks. And then six weeks of radiation, five days a week.

She only has a few more treatments left this week and hopefully that will take care of this brave young lady's problem. Meanwhile, she has been an inspiration to all of us. All heroes don't show their bravery during wartime. Those who heroically battle cancer are just as brave.

And with God's help, Eleanor will win. She is already a winner in my book.

SHE HAS INSISTED on working during the entire ordeal. "I don't want to sit around and feel sorry for myself. I need to stay busy."

She'd have an occasional energy lag, but not too often. This young lady likes to shop and has led her mother on a merry chase through the malls. On one of these weekend trips, which left her mother breathless, wilted and exhausted, she explained: "I need to be doing something. Besides I want to see and do everything. This has all reminded me how important it is to feel good and not be worried about your health."

Eleanor is a beautiful lady, and a father has been more worried about her hair loss than she has. "This wig is easier to fool with than my own hair," she says, passing off my concern.

Her mother asked: "Do you want to see how her hair looks now that it's coming back?"

"Not yet," said this chicken. "I'll wait a few more months until it's all back."

It has been an ordeal for us all. No one member of a family is singled out when cancer or any other sickness strikes. We are all involved and concerned.

Daughter, we love you very much and you know it. We also admire your courage, determination and zest for living.

We told you so again at the family dinner where we congratulated you on your fighting spirit, your progress and the fact your treatments are coming to an end.

Hopefully, God Himself will take note of your strong desire to get well and live a long and healthy life. Maybe He has a special medal for those brave people who so dearly love the life He has given them — and are determined to fight for it.

A Time Machine That Wouldn't Fly

I SAW HER IN A SHOWROOM window in 1956, and it was love at first sight.

She wore a shrimp and off-white colored coat and her lines were a joy to behold. At the time I was introduced to her, I didn't know anything about her background or what kind of a "heart" she had.

I learned later she had a Packard engine with a 10 to 1 compression ratio and that she was one of the most powerful passenger cars on the road. She was a knockout, and I fell in love with her and took her home to show to my family the same day we met.

You'd have to see her to appreciate her beauty, her sleekness and with it all her good taste. She was a head-turner, and I reveled at every glance cast her way. I wasn't jealous and liked to introduce her to my friends and colleagues. They were impressed.

At the time I didn't know that although she was from a proud family lineage, that in a few years her line would become extinct.

She was a Studebaker Golden Hawk, and not to be confused with any other of the less haughty and powerful Hawks such as the Silver and Sky Hawk, who were not in her class.

Her streamlined body had been specially coiffured by a noted auto designer, and she was ahead of her time in many ways. Aside from the breath-taking cosmetic effect of this haughty beauty, who looked down her nose at the road from her rather long, patrician hood, she was an astounding performer.

She heeded my slightest request with a surge that rocked my head back against the real leather seats. She had a sultry growl of a voice that I loved to hear.

A friend who is the most knowledgeable car nut around said the Golden Hawk would do a "true 125 miles an hour" and then set out to prove it. On more than several occasions I tried to see how spirited she was and how far I could push her but luckily she and I never had a scrap or scratch.

I TAKE A PERSONAL INTEREST in every car I've ever had. Each has her own individual personality and traits. A car to me is more than a utilitarian object that gets me from one point to another. It is a wondrous creation from the mind of God's own creation.

Each car also connects me with certain phases and events of our life. Betty and I become attached to cars and hate to part with them.

But that Golden Hawk will never be forgotten — the way she looked and the way she handled, and at high speeds and on mountain curves.

She took me to my first national convention and then to numerous others. Even as she got older, she still turned heads. On New York's Broadway, she caught the jaded eyes of onlookers, and she got admiring stares in Chicago and Florida.

She took me back and forth to Nashville for the meetings of the Legislature and didn't complain about those treacherous, tortuous mountain roads before the interstate was built.

In looking back, I marvel at the nerve, energy and horsepower we both had in those days. We lived on the edge too many times. We took too many chances, but we were lucky and came out unscathed.

Later, with the wear and tear of years and mileage, I reluctantly got another car, but I kept the Hawk in the family by giving her to one of our sons.

But the inevitable finally happened and someone else got my proud beauty. I never knew who it was. She was traded in. I don't want to know because he wouldn't love her the way I did.

ABOUT TWO WEEKS AGO, I dreamed I had parked my Golden Hawk on one of the levels of a huge parking garage. Apparently I had forgotten which level it was. So, I ran up one floor and down another. I would think I had spotted her in her lovely coat, but when I got near, I was disappointed to find it was some other car.

This went on and on. I was exhausted. I don't know how long dream segments last, but it was long enough to fill me with pain and longing. Where had I parked that car I loved so much?

Where indeed had time and car gone and was my search for this beautiful vehicle a fleeting, wishful look back at younger and more vigorous days for car and owner? It doesn't take a Joseph to arrive at such an interpretation.

Searching for my Golden Hawk was like trying to fly a time machine, one that wouldn't fly back. I finally awoke and was sad and pensive for longer than a while.

Those indeed were golden days, for car and driver.

We can look back, but we can't have them back.

HAVE YOU EVER STUCK
YOUR NECK OUT?

"HOW COULD AN ENTIRE NATION allow that to happen?" asked the young man.

He was referring to the atrocities that occurred in Germany when Hitler was in power and millions of people were imprisoned, tortured and killed.

Yes, he had read and heard of reasons: A nation in economic and political shambles, one in need of restored national pride, one in search of identity and leadership, and one seeking a scapegoat for the chaotic predicament it was in.

But he wasn't satisfied with these "surface" excuses. "This still doesn't explain a nation's willingness to go along with a madman's extermination of millions of innocent people, including Jews, Poles and many other ethnic groups, plus anyone who stood in his way."

Of course it doesn't explain such a heinous mass extermination of people.

He also wondered if such unthinkable atrocities could have happened anywhere else, in any other country.

He was referred to the Spanish Inquisition and the Crusades for starters. "But it wasn't as bad back then," he observed. "Not as many people were killed."

Right. Torture and killing were refined by the time Hitler

came into power. Much "progress" had been made in the fiendish business of exterminating entire races of people.

"I still don't understand," said the young man, "how people can just stand by and allow such terrible things to happen. How can they live with themselves if they didn't try to do something to stop what was going on?"

Some people did try to help, he was told. And some paid a price for their willingness to put their lives on the line. Most, however, went along with Hitler's "master race" theory and methods.

THE WORD "LIVE," which was used by the sensitive young man, is the key word in his probe of a nation of people's willingness to follow orders designed to decimate entire races of people.

Most people did so for fear of doing otherwise. Freedom and one's very life were at risk if they didn't get in step with the goose-steppers. Of course some enjoyed their new-found role of authority and power, as heinous as the methods were.

We respect the young man's shock at this bloody chapter of history, which took place not too long ago. His father spent more than half a decade in the U.S. Army along with millions of others fighting the armies of Hitler. So history is still very much alive for him.

We've heard many young men ask such questions and it augurs well for a country for its youth to be shocked at the bloody history of Germany under Hitler.

I asked the same questions during my wartime service in Germany during World War II. And there were times when I hated the Germans not only for what they had done to millions of innocent people, but for what they were doing to the life of this individual.

With every bone-freezing day and night on the field and every battle that took lives and left the rest of us grateful to still be alive but so miserably cold and shaken that the alternative seemed a way out, this soldier and other soldiers hated the Germans more.

An example of this overabundance of venom was seen when a little, roundfaced blond boy asked for a piece of "confetti" in a captured German town.

"I'll give you some confetti," said the American sergeant, as he flaunted a large chunk of chocolate. Just before the three- or four-year-old child could reach the candy, the sergeant let it drop into the ever-stinking mud and with his heel ground it into nothingness.

The child looked at the spot where the candy was dropped and then looked at the soldier with a "why did you do that?" expression of puzzled innocence.

The ex-sergeant said he can still see "that child's face." He has blotted out many unpleasant war memories, but this one has stayed with him. It personifies man's inhumanity and hatred during war.

IT WAS MANY YEARS before I could become more objec–tive about the German people's role under Hitler. I thought, "Maybe there is a genetic flaw in the makeup of this cruel, warlike race which seems to unduly love its armies and flashy uniforms and martial music even under the sway of a demented dictator."

It is easier to condemn an entire race of people. Hitler did this, and it almost worked for him. But then the saner atmosphere of civilian life gives one an occasional chance to ponder and think through various certainties that were once embraced. The young man's aforementioned discussion of the moral obligations to stop a Hitler causes one to reflect on lesser battlefields with considerably less risk to those who would stand up for what they considered to be the right thing.

Does one do the right thing even if one is only risking promotion or job security? The answer is usually "no." That is the truthful answer in most cases.

If your government were in the hands of a dictator, would you speak out at the risk of your freedom or life? Would you offer to hide and give shelter to those whom your government deemed as traitors and enemies of the state, since this would definitely mean giving up your life and that of your family if you were detected?

NOW, STANDING UP for the right thing is not beginning to sound simplistic. It also wasn't during the war years.

Back to the "battleground" of civilian life: Someone in your office is being mistreated, not just by a person of equal rank but by a supervisor or boss who has the authority to make the going very rough.

The mistreatment is obviously unfair, and you should speak up even if you catch flak for it. But do you? You don't have freedom and life at risk, but you are looking down the road at your own opportunities. It was only your job, but you didn't come to the aid of a fellow human who was being mistreated.

Is the comparison there? Does that take away just a little smugness and self-righteousness and the premise you would have protested the bloody and mad machinations of a Hitler even if your life was at stake?

The truth is, if someone is on "the list," most of us will give him a wide berth, even if it's the office list.

WHEN WAS THE LAST TIME you braced the boss or fore-man because he was unfair and cruel to a good worker and especially a good friend of yours? Or do you just wince and offer words of commiseration and empathy to the one who has been publicly excoriated and humiliated? And this of course is done out of earshot and sight of the boss.

No use in both of you being on the black list. Isn't that right? What good would that serve?

Or do you just give a wide berth to the person on the list, thereby keeping you out of the line of fire? He is being mis-treated, ostracized and shunned, but life must go on. What else can you do, you ask.

And this is not even a life and death situation.

People often rise to great heights of heroism and personal sacrifice. But more often fear of reprisal for ourselves and our families makes cowards out of most of us and keeps us from getting involved. In part, this is how we allow such things to happen.

Meanwhile let's be aware of injustice whether it be of the Hitler variety — or cruelty, hatred and intolerance on these beloved shores of ours.

A Letter To 'Kids'
Who Have Kids

AN OPEN LETTER TO OUR THREE CHILDREN:
Dear kids:

For some quirky reason, I find this an easier way to express my feelings on certain subjects, especially those concerning you. Don't ask me why, but sometimes my innermost feelings get stuck somewhere between my vocal chords and my Adam's apple and they aren't articulated.

So why am I going public rather than writing to you privately? Because I believe most parents have the same concerns, feelings of inadequacy and even guilt in regard to parenting.

Also, as you know, none of us is a prolific letter-writer. And somehow an unemotional and unblushing computer tends to take the awkwardness out of being revealingly candid. But because this will be read by others than yourselves, I'll try to keep the "letter" from becoming too corny.

IN A COLUMN I wrote on this subject some years ago, I noted most mistakes parents make in the upbringing of their young are unintentional and that children should not continue to hold this human failing against their parents.

If the hurt was unintentional, why not be forgiving? It is a widely accepted fact that even a dog or a cat distinguishes between being stumbled over and being kicked. My point was that since pets seem to understand the subtle difference between accidentally and intentionally inflicting pain, one wonders why this subtlety should escape one's own children.

I call for amnesty for the stumbling older generation and for parents in particular. Sure, we've made our share of mistakes, and we are not the first generation to do this. But your generation was probably the first to put so much emphasis on how those mistakes shaped your "formative years."

Even as I reread the column, I can see how my views have changed and mellowed. For instance, consider this paragraph:

"I've never been one to rush the years, but it would almost be worth hurrying time ahead to watch my kids raise their kids without any mistakes . . . without even stumbling."

So that time is now here. Between you there are now four grandchildren, and naturally we think they are the greatest. We also think you young people are fine parents and are probably making fewer mistakes than we made. I know you boys are more cognizant of the importance of the father's role.

You show it by your patience and love of your children and the quality time you spend with them. Maybe priorities have changed, but you seem more aware of the fleeting nature of childhood and the importance of spending time with your boys. And your wives and our daughter also have terrific patience and realize that childhood is a magical, transient time.

I guess what it all boils down to is this: When we see the kind of loving parents you are, we are reassured that whatever it was we didn't do exactly right must not have been too bad or traumatic for you. The way you have turned out has made us proud. We are also proud of the "dividends" from our original investment.

LOOKING BACK, I can see a trail of stumbling footprints — my own. I should have been more tolerant and patient of you little people. But I was brought up in the no-nonsense school of "do as you are told" or else.

Even so, I will give myself at least a passing mark for easing up on you three as we all grew older and wiser. Somewhere along the line, I learned there was more to raising three youngsters than making them toe the line. There could also be the fun and laughter of games and jokes and song-filled trips.

I am also reminded of the times your exasperated mother (a housewife then) would tell me of the mischief you had gotten into during the day and then regret telling me and implore me not to lay a hand on you. "After all, they are just children," she would say on numerous occasions. And she was just naturally being a protective mother who really didn't want to get her children in trouble, especially with their father.

I believe we worked longer hours back then, never turning down overtime assignments. This was probably a spinoff from the Great Depression we experienced as young people. Anyway, allow me to rationalize that being tired was a factor in my being irritable on occasions. But I will also use the "formative years" line and claim that I too got quite a bit of "no-nonsense" treatment from my father during those years.

Maybe that is why some of that discipline literally rubbed off on you.

I AM PROUD you have a strong sense of job and family responsibility. I am also impressed that you young people have a keen sense of priorities. Unlike some, you place health and family ahead of less important things that seem to preoccupy other less discerning people.

I have seen your concern when a child is not feeling well. That
is a bond that we share with every caring parent who has ever
lived on this earth.

I have also seen that look of pride when one of those little
ones did something that was funny, cute or "very advanced." We
understand. We've been there — at elementary and high school
graduations and college functions and when "very good" report
cards were brought home.

Kids, on the subject of report cards and other things, try not to
make the mistake of comparing one child's progress with that
of the other. They are individuals with their own unique talents
and rate of physical and mental growth. I finally learned that.

A college diploma is also something to be proud of and we've
heard you already discussing money for college. I don't believe
when I was your age I was looking that far ahead, which bears out
our belief that you were precocious kids in many ways.

YOU'VE NOTICED I HAVEN'T criticized you for anything,
and I'm not going to at this late date. Why argue with success?
Seems like you're bringing up those youngsters just fine, and all
of you seem to be having a lot of fun in between the shots and
things that go wrong with kids every now and then. You seem to
be finding a point of moderation: not too hasty to correct and
not too lax.

If I had it to do all over again, I would have gone easier on my
criticism of you, especially for little things that hardly mattered. I
would not have been as rigid and demanding. These are children, not small adults.

I would also have been less critical of a young mother taking
on the demanding role of fulltime homemaker and trying to
please a demanding husband and a critical mother-in-law.

Back then wives went out of their way to stay in the good

graces of the husband's mother even if they were rebuffed more often than not. I was the only child and in my case not even royalty would have been my mother's idea of "the one" for me.

The other day I was touched when your mother handed me an annual memorial candle and gently said: "It's time to light this for Mom." That's the kind of mother you kids have. She reminds me each year that I should "light this" for my father or for my mother. There are no bitter words. Just concern for her husband's feelings and respect for his departed parents.

My dad dearly loved your mother and the feeling was reciprocated.

THE OTHER DAY I heard a song that said something about "Time, don't run out on me." No, I'm not ill as far as I know and hopefully I'll be around for quite a while. But that song again reminded me that life doesn't go on forever and that I won't be here as long as I have been.

It also reminded me to write this letter and let you know how I feel about you and how proud we are of you and your young families.

Keep on enjoying each other and your children as much as you possibly can. You are on the right track. As the years go by, you will more and more realize that people need each other. It is hard to make it through life alone.

Sure, making a good living is important. So is living each day to the hilt.

Remember what I told you years ago when you complained about that upcoming exam: "Don't let it scare you. Just consider it a challenge and do the best you can." Life is like that.

That's it for now, kids. Your mother and I love you and yours very much.

With love,

Dad.

A FEW LIKES
AND DISLIKES

HERE ARE SOME TRUTHFUL LIKES AND DISLIKES:

A child's uncontrived smile, outstretched arms and other indications he is delighted to see you or be with you, make one feel wonderfully warm and rewarded.

The sheer honesty that exudes from this little person is humbling and reassuring, especially by comparison with the often phony greetings and feigned delight of grownups.

For instance, "darling" has been used so often in a non-meaning manner that it has lost its original meaning of endearment. In the next few minutes, that same "darling" can be savaged by the effusive greeter as she takes her apart in a discussion with another piranha.

You'd think this kind of two-facedness would be a warning to others that if it can happen to one person it can happen to another and another until it's full-circle time. Not to believe this is to be dishonest with one's self.

I ADMIRE THOSE who have a strong sense of loyalty to their friends. They step in to help or defend a friend, regardless of the circumstances or the status of the defamer.

This too has become, to a great extent, an anachronism.

Nowadays there are such things to consider as not offending someone who might be willing to help you or who might put a stumbling block in your way.

So, when your friend is described in uncomplimentary three-letter initials, you come to his defense by replying: "But he's not such a bad — once you get to know him." Boy, that's really sticking your neck out for a friend.

And of course there are those who consider friendship a wonderful thing until they're called on for help. All of a sudden it's back to business as usual. "Besides, if you were a real friend you wouldn't have put me, your friend, on the spot by asking for a favor."

Someone was impressed with the number of people who greeted a newsman during a social function. She said, "I'll bet you have hundreds of friends."

He replied, "I can count them on one hand, not using my thumb."

"You've got to be kidding," she said. "Look how many people know you and like you."

"Maybe you mean acquaintances," he said. "I've got hundreds of acquaintances, but I only have about three or four friends . . . and I can count myself lucky I have that many."

Go ahead and count. It's all right to use your fingers. One hand is all you'll need.

I LIKE PEOPLE of goodwill and good humor. I don't like to be around those who have a jaundiced outlook on life and are mean-tempered and mean-spirited. These abrasive, negative individuals can pull you down and literally put a damper on your day, if you allow it.

I've noticed that live-and-let-live people have a good sense of humor to cushion against life's vagaries and troubles. Being around them is like warming yourself by a cheerful, crackling fireplace. No one gets burned. You just get warmed.

I like people who have been able to keep their feet on the ground during notable periods of success and despite the praise and fuss made over them. These are the "big ones" who stand out like giants in the land of pygmies.

I dislike and pity the snobs who are so insecure they can only fuel their ego by chopping up others like kindling wood. What they lack in confidence they usually make up in prejudice. I haven't met a person of substance and stature who was a snob and needed to whittle away at the ego of others.

I LIKE GENUINE PEOPLE. They don't put on airs.

I dislike phonies who insult your intelligence and your credulity.

I like people who respect the dignity of the other person regardless of race, creed and color.

I dislike those who try to run roughshod over others, including waitresses and anyone less powerful and less likely to retaliate. I despise bullies and admit I applaud when they get their comeuppance. That's not nice, but how sweet it is.

I like people who have a strong work ethic. I very much dislike goldbricks, slackers and slocums.

I like people who listen to what is being said. I try to avoid bores and those who like the sound of their own voices far too much.

I like tolerant people with a sense of humor who can also laugh at themselves. I'm leery of humorless people who take themselves too seriously.

I like freedom seekers. I hate dictators and dislike freedom being taken for granted.

I like kind and considerate people. This world would be intolerable without them.

WHEN OUR DAUGHTER CAME BACK 'HOME'

OUR DAUGHTER ELEANOR came back home again this past Friday night. But this time it wasn't for a visit. This time it was to stay.

We would have done anything for her not to come home this way, although for years we had urged her to return here to be with her family who dearly love her.

Eleanor, known as Ellie to many friends and relatives, was buried Sunday, two days after being flown in from Memphis on a Med-Flight ambulance, accompanied by her mother and a brother.

Her mother said Ellie confided she didn't want to come back earlier "because I don't want you and Dad to see me suffering."

Writing this column is my first major attempt to step back out of the valley of darkness into the light of a living world. There are hundreds of ways this could be written, but not one way would be without wrenching pain.

Only those who have lost a child can fully understand the loss of such a priceless gift. There is something highly unnatural about a child dying before a parent. It is out of sequence. It doesn't make any sense at all.

My wife and I have asked the usual question: "Why?" And especially when that person exuded an aura of sweetness, gentleness, kindness and giving and wouldn't deliberately hurt another person, even if it meant hurt for herself.

We haven't been given any satisfactory answers. I don't believe there are logical answers that can be understood by mere mortal and that can offer real comfort. I've talked to various theologians of different faiths and they agree there are no easy answers to the question: "Why?"

THE HEALING PROCESS must begin within us, even as we hurt. Time, family and friends help ease the pain, but we know it will never entirely go away.

But then we remember the excruciating pain Ellie suffered, and we marvel at her bravery and survival instinct and how she clung to life even to her last breath, and with a minimum of complaint. Brave little lady!

Before Ellie's ill-fated bout with breast cancer, I thought it was trite and a platitude when someone said: "He (or she) is now better off. There won't be any more pain."

No, there won't be, baby. And for that, at least, your mother and I are grateful.

Dear reader, I don't want to be maudlin and unload on you, although being able to write about our precious daughter is a form of catharsis for me.

In helping us to share this awful burden, maybe someone else can find a modicum of comfort. Maybe a cancer-fighting contribution can be made.

There is a universality in grief which we have all experienced in some form. Even the winners among us are born to lose what we cherish most.

But when it happens — especially in regard to a child — it doubly comes as a shock, and the questions and the sense of unfairness and frustration well up in us to the point of anger.

But even when our faith is rocked, we feel a Divine Presence that enables us to heal a little each day. Something beyond our understanding takes place when friends, co-workers, neighbors, relatives and even those we don't personally know, pour out their love and sympathy to us.

Cards and letters by the hundreds, flowers and food-offerings have inundated us. So have phone calls and offers to visit and help comfort us.

There has to be a Divine Spirit behind such an outpouring of love and concern.

ELLIE FIRST DISCOVERED she had breast cancer in April of last year, and she underwent surgery for the removal of several lumps. However, a couple of doctors expressed concern she had waited too long before she had a base-line mammogram.

She was treated with chemotherapy and radiation but the persistent killer had apparently gotten a head start. Her age, 43, also put her at risk of having a highly aggressive cancer.

I believe she realized the extent of her illness and she tried to get the most out of each day. Shortly after her operation, she insisted on working here part-time, and shopping was also high on her agenda.

She recuperated here and was concerned about my flagging spirits. "Make Dad quit worrying," she'd tell her mother. "That's not going to help any of us."

Recently she came back for a minor cosmetic operation. Shortly after the surgery she was wheeled out to the car and then immediately walked back into the hospital to start visiting other patients.

This past April she began having pain which seemed to travel all over her body. However, numerous scans and x-rays failed to reveal the cause. The pain was already intense and she was taking medicine to alleviate it.

She limited the potent dosage so she could be alert on her secretary-receptionist job. But then it was back again to Baptist Memorial Hospital East in Memphis. More tests, and pain-filled days later, our fears and the fears of her doctor were confirmed.

"She has one of the most aggressive cancers I have ever seen," her doctor said. "It doesn't follow any of the patterns that cancer usually takes."

Her mother, her two brothers and I witnessed her final suffering for what seemed an eternity. It was about two weeks and she was given as much morphine as could be legally provided.

"What is wrong with me," she asked during one of her rare lucid moments. The rest of the time she slept fitfully and every now and then almost peacefully.

Just the act of turning her in her bed brought forth cries of anguish as she awoke from her medicine-induced sleep.

I'm not good at handling suffering, especially that of my daughter. I often took refuge from this ongoing nightmare as I shut the door of a room that had been vacated across the hall.

I ONLY THOUGHT I KNEW the agony of those who have lost children in various ways. I really thought I knew the extent of their grief.

I apologize for being so presumptive. I've suffered the loss of parents and friends, and sure it hurts. But the loss of a child is a searing pain which I cannot describe. I hope to God you will never experience this kind of agony, this ultimate pain.

The questions persist. Why did this have to happen? Why did someone so young and sweet and loving have to suffer so? These and other questions gnaw at me, and I don't have any answers.

But then I remember the fact I can even function is a miracle of sorts. And the healing process is a miracle, as is the outpouring of love we have received.

I hesitated to write this column so early. But such as it is, it is now written, and I didn't think I would be able to write so soon after we buried Ellie.

We all have lost and will lose and hopefully Eleanor's death will serve to remind us and others how lucky we are to have held on to this gift of God for as long as we did.

Hopefully, someone will appreciate these "gifts" more and get more out of each day in their busy lives they hurry through without realizing time is also hurrying.

I AM NOT an "organized religion" person but I do believe in a Divine Being even though I wonder and still wonder, Why? Why did this have to happen to Ellie? Why did God allow this terrible thing to happen to her?

For that matter, why do we walk through so much darkness and occasionally have fleeting glimpses of light? Is it so we will better appreciate the preciousness of life?

But His presence must be in allowing us to hold on before and during Ellie's funeral and to be able to get up the next day and even function. It must be in my wife's courage and strength and the personal sacrifices made by Ellie's two brothers, Barry and Steve, and in the dedication and kindness shown to Eleanor and us by nurses and sitters around the clock.

As I sat and grieved on a maternity ward window ledge, a buxom woman patient, out for a walk, asked: "Are you here for your new grandchild?" I told her: "I wish." I said our daughter was dying. Ellie was the only cancer patient on a floor reserved for maternity cases. She wanted it that way for obvious reasons and the doctor consented.

The cries of the infants and the congratulatory flower wreaths celebrating the incoming of new life were in stark contrast to the imminent departure of our daughter's life.

The motherly-type stranger surrounded me with a comforting, loving hug. She held me for a long moment. Her spontaneous embrace got to me. I shed tears for the hundredth time.

A FEW MOMENTS of consciousness that stand out:.

So much hurt and pain in Ellie's bewildered eyes . . . that beautiful, little-girl face, she always was beautiful . . . mumbling something about being late for school and whether she passed her test . . . Steve and Barry and I kissing her feverish forehead and reassuring her . . . Betty telling her during a rare sitting-up moment: "You know Momma loves you. Can I give you a kiss?" A barely audible "Yes," and then, "Do you want to kiss me?" "Yes," Ellie replied and whispered, "Let's do it again."

More standouts: A cousin's, Dr. Joseph Parker's, compassionate help and repeated visits . . . The constant hospital room vigil of Steve . . . The support system provided by Barry and Steve and their respective wives back home . . . The unselfish friendship and support of David, a friend of Ellie's . . . Betty, who is not quite five feet tall, tiptoeing over Ellie's bed-railing trying to kiss our girl.

When it became apparent Eleanor had only a short time to live, Betty insisted we fly Ellie home while she was still alive. "I'll go with her. I don't want her to come back home alone." After a race against time, the Med-Flight ambulance out of Little Rock was obtained. A nurse and paramedic were on board, but a co-pilot had to be "bumped" so Steve could also fly with his sister.

There was no hesitation on the part of Betty and Steve to fly back with her. On the flight she became restless and the paramedic smoothed her brow and urged her: "Hold on Ellie, you'll be home in a few minutes."

She arrived at Memorial Hospital at 11:30 p.m. Daughters-In-

Law LeNet and Hollee were waiting. Ellie died at 5:30 the next morning. Sunday we attended her funeral.

Barry had driven me home Saturday and provided me with almost non-stop couch therapy for seven hours. He was a captive listener as a grieving father wondered why this had happened.

Barry blamed nature for Eleanor's suffering and death. "It was a case of cells gone crazy."

As the beautiful mountains past Monteagle came into view, I said: "I believe I could admire nature more if she weren't so vicious."

"I believe 'indifferent' is the word," said my spiritually-oriented son.

ELLIE TOUCHED THE LIVES of many people. She was a beautiful person.

Her mother and I want to make sure she didn't die in vain. Her suffering and death have got to have some meaning. We will see to that. Otherwise our entire existence is just an absurdity.

Last Mother's Day, Eleanor wrote on a card: "Dear Mom, the older I get the more I understand the pleasures and frustrations of being a mother. I feel like we are probably closer than ever before, and I am only sorry it took so long to become not only Mother and Daughter but also friends.

"I love both of you, Mom and Dad, very much. Have a wonderful day and I will see you soon. Love, Eleanor."

Betty will always treasure that card. Appropriately, I just found a pocket card in my wallet which I had forgotten about. It said, "Father of the Year Award belongs to you." On the back: "No doubt about it!" Signed, "Your Daughter."

I'll forever treasure this card, especially on this Father's Day.

Goodbye, sweet daughter. We'll always miss you and your gentle, kind and loving ways.

You are gone, our pretty baby, but we'll always cherish our memories of you. You were a very special "gift."

GIVE HIM TIME TO 'LIGHTEN UP'

DEAR READERS, PLEASE INDULGE ME yet one more time.

Believe me, I had made a sincere effort to write a lighter column this week. It was my intention to do so.

"Look," I reasoned, "Sunday is a day to relax and unwind and read the Sunday comics and be with your family and generally heal and be fresher for the workaday world which starts again tomorrow."

For a lot of people, Sunday is also a day to become spiritually recharged and to slow down long enough to appreciate the miracle of life and God's bountiful earth.

Besides, I thought, enough is enough on any given subject, even if it is about the tragedy of losing a daughter and friends. Every grownup has had his or her share of tragedy. Ease up on your readers. You've leaned enough.

So let me see what I can come up with. Throughout many years, I have written on hundreds of subjects and have felt in touch with readers. So, what shall I write about?

Potential subjects are numerous and varied, but they hardly generate a spark of interest at this particular time.

This is not good. I find that in order for writing to have a ring of truth, it is better to write about something uppermost in one's mind. Something you urgently want to communicate.

When you write just to fill space, it will have a fill-in-the-blanks tone and readers will easily pick up on the lack of inspiration behind this sort of forced writing.

They can tell a column with spontaneity and one that is strained. They can tell if a column is written by a typewriter or computer and not from the heart.

But events and subjects that had previously seemed important to me have currently been relegated to the category of "so what?" My mind is literally riveted to the tragic happenings of the past few weeks in which we lost our only daughter and two friends.

It was a triple whammy, and I'm still reeling from the combination of blows. If they didn't floor me, they had me hanging on the ropes with very little fight left in me.

If you'll pardon the analogy, in the words of an old, country preacher:

"The Lord done put a hammerlock on me."

THERE ARE THOSE who will take issue with this kind of theology. But hopefully we'll be occasionally released from this "hold" in order to be more interested in what is going on around us and to again write about a variety of subjects.

I need to be able and willing to look beyond our great loss and to consider the things, thoughts and events which make up our everyday lives.

They are important, and I have been reminded life does go on. I realize I have much to be grateful for, including my wife, our two sons and my friends and family.

I hope this reentry into the world happens soon. I know my daughter and my two friends would want me and my wife to get on with our lives. But even this time, we won't burden you with as much personal pain of losing a child and friends.

Instead, we want to discuss the spinoff, the reminders of the basic goodness of people, of the friends, acquaintances and people we don't even know.

Their outpouring of sympathy in many forms has been a real eye opener and comfort to me and to Betty. People I would normally shake hands with now want to hold and comfort and show their deep concern.

And just as we are all different in appearance and personality, each one of us has his or her own way of expressing sympathy.

Some write cards and letters and make phone calls. Some send flowers, fruit and food. Some make contributions. Some also visit and make follow-up phone calls.

SOME HAVE A HARD TIME saying what is on their minds and in their hearts and simply look at you as they hold your hand and express their feelings through their eyes. Some find themselves inept to communicate at such a time and their awkwardness is also quite touching.

A giant of a man I had never seen came up to my desk a few days ago, put his arm around me and said: "You'll be all right."

As he turned to walk away, I asked him: "What is your name, sir?"

"I'll see you again," he said. "We'll talk again." He waved as he walked away.

And then there are the huggers. They literally wrap themselves around you and your heart as they gently pat you on the back.

With many, it is more than just thinking they know how one feels. Many of them know from experience. They have also lost daughters and sons and friends. "I know, I know, I know," they say as they relive their own losses.

I have been amazed at the revealing contents of hundreds of letters and cards we have received here at the newspaper and at our home. I never realized so many people had also lost children.

One woman wrote she had lost three children over the years, two in an automobile accident and one because of leukemia, and "the hurt will never go away.

"Time heals, it doesn't restore," she wrote.

Another lady called to express sympathy. "I know how you and Betty feel," she said. "We also lost a darling daughter to cancer, and we will never get over it."

"When did your daughter die?" I asked.

There was a long pause. When she regained composure, she replied:

"Eighteen years ago."

UNTIL ELEANOR DIED, I never realized so many people had been down that same road. We were now walking in their moccasins, and we truly understood.

A mother who said her 30-year-old daughter died in a head-on automobile collision two years ago offered this thought:

"I know how it hurts. But try and remember that you and I were blessed with having them for the years we did. Some people have never known the joy (and problems) of having children. At least we have memories that we can hold on to."

She wrote, "Our only daughter was seven months pregnant when she was taken from us. She was a wonderful gift. So would have been our grandchild."

The daughter was also their only child.

The word "gift" keeps appearing in the letters we are still receiving. Somehow this serves to alleviate some of our pain when we ask, "Why?"

Others say they have also asked "why" and have received no

answer but have found solace in the reminder their children were "gifts."

A local judge wrote he and his wife realize the devastation that takes place when a child that has been loved and protected from hurt and suffering then suffers and dies after she becomes an adult.

He said, "The memories with her that you recalled in the article made us pause to think about our own children, and we realized again the tenuous hold we have on them. They indeed are gifts and belong first to God . . . "

Time and gain this theme is sounded. It seems to help.

I HAVE BEEN AWARE for a long time that eulogies don't include bottom-line figures.

I have yet to hear a preacher or rabbi extol the fact the deceased had a great knack for playing the stock market and knew how to buy low and sell high.

I have never heard a man of the cloth cite the person who was being buried as having a net worth of "X" dollars.

I HAVE heard preachers praise civic and business leaders for their competitiveness while retaining the human touch which led them to be highly charitable with the money they made.

Their worth as people was measured in what they did with their earnings, not how they managed to accumulate same.

We lost a lovely daughter a few weeks ago. At her funeral no mention was made about her financial status. Her Memphis savings and checking accounts were quite nominal. Her bills will no doubt deplete this modest sum.

However, the emphasis was on how she had touched the lives of her family and others with her sweet disposition, her willingness to help others and her unusually kind spirit.

Shortly before Ellie died, we had lost a good friend from our old YMCA days, Alex Guerry. He was a widely known business-man and civic leader.

Shortly after Ellie died, we lost our friend and publisher, Roy McDonald.

Both of these highly successful men did much for their community and for those who needed their help. They would seek out such persons.

Ellie was 43 when she died. Alex Guerry was 72, and Mr. Roy was 88.

Each one was different and occupied different roles in life. Yet each touched more people than we realized.

That was their true worth. It was pointed out in the eulogies given them.

WE ARE TRYING TO ANSWER as many cards and letters as possible and to thank you for them and for phone calls and love offerings of fruits, food and flowers.

But the remarkable amount of consideration, sympathy and love shown us will make the completion of our thank-you notes impossible for a long time.

If you don't hear from us, it isn't because we are not touched by your kindness. You have helped more than you possibly realize.

Thanks again and again. It helps by taking the focus off one's own tragedy when we learn of the tragedies of others. It also shows that the human spirit is indomitable and that one can live through such losses, although there is no forgetting.

But then we don't want to forget. We want to hold on to those dear memories of our beautiful daughter and better days.

But as I promised, I will try to "get on" with another subject next week. With God's help, I will.

THE OTHER DAY my wife noted that a large motel was being planned adjacent to Hamilton Place Mall.

Ellie loved to travel and shop and even after she became ill, she would encourage her mother to go shopping with her. Not necessarily to buy, but to at least shop. She particularly loved Hamilton Place. Betty is not much of a shopper. If she could, she would have someone else shop for her.

"There's nothing like this in Memphis," said Ellie, who considered herself a Chattanoogan who just happened to work in Memphis.

"With the motel in Hamilton Place, wouldn't she have something else to brag about her home town?" remarked her mother. "I can just see her looking it over and telling me I should go see how nice it is."

We both smiled at the thought. We haven't had too much to smile about lately ever since we buried our pretty little shopper.

Hopefully, the healing process will continue for us.

Thanks again, dear readers and friends and everyone else we've heard from.

Thanks for helping us through this.

WHEN 'ORDINARY' BECOMES EXTRAORDINARY

NOTHING IS ORDINARY if you don't think it is. No one's life is ordinary if the person living it doesn't think so.

If you're clicking along in your familiar and normal manner, don't downgrade yourself into believing you are living a dull, boring and ordinary existence. Nothing may be further from the truth.

More often than not the status quo is desirable. But we get in a rut, take it for granted and assume everyone but us is having a ball.

The same old thing means different things to different people.

Driving to work every morning in heavy traffic may be a hassle to you, but not having a job to go to is a bigger one for someone who desperately needs and wants to work. What may appear to be ordinary to one person could be a dream come true for someone else.

DON'T BE AMONG those non-perceptive people who take health, family and good fortune for granted and believe the other guy is the only lucky one.

Not only have they not examined their own lives, they haven't observed what is going on around them. Compared to others being badly bashed by fate and circumstance, they are the lucky ones and don't know it.

It's this taking for granted that literally takes the excitement and appreciation out of life.

A kid who is used to getting almost anything he asks for will not be as excited about his new, sleek, expensive sports car as the boy or girl who got a used first car with the help of his or her parents' down payment. Never mind the car is six years old and has taken its share of bruises.

The affluent youth looks on his car as something ordinary and due him. He won't have to work to meet the payments and the insurance. He expects these good things to happen to him as part of the "good life" his family has gotten him used to.

The proud owner of the used car is more likely to appreciate it, although he might make a mental note to one day be the owner of a sleek, new sports car.

And when that day does arrive, there won't be anything ordinary about it since he bought it.

HUMAN NATURE BEING what is is, apparently it takes doing without to appreciate what we have.

There is no doubt no one can enjoy a good meal like a hungry man. The operative word is "hungry." A peanut butter sandwich can be delicious. If you are hungry, it won't taste ordinary.

Those who have taste for life don't feel they have a special dispensation to receive the blessings of life. They know life is full of twists and turns, and they try to enjoy it as much as possible. They do believe life is for living, and when they sit down at the feast they take a bigger bite.

They give thanks for each meal and each good thing that happens to them. These optimistic realists know at best life is a precariously balanced gift and is too precious to fritter away and be bored with.

They know human beings arrive on this earth with no contract. There is no guarantee of any kind, including health, longevity or prosperity.

Perceptive people also realize there is nothing commonplace or ordinary about the miracle of life.

SOME YEARS AGO, we enjoyed the friendship of a philanthropist who also happened to be a multimillionaire. On our dining-out occasions, he took great delight in recalling the adventures and the hard work of his immigrant parents.

Others close to him weren't that keen on his recounting his parents' struggle to feed their hungry brood. He was reminded, "No one wants to hear about those days. Let's talk about something more exciting."

But he would not be derailed. Turning to us, he asked: "You find this interesting, don't you?"

"Most interesting." We had our own immigrant family of which we are proud.

Because of his background and his success, the philanthropist saw nothing commonplace or ordinary about forebears who took great risks and made numerous sacrifices which in turn enabled succeeding generations to live much, much better lives.

I also view these latter-day pioneers as being anything but ordinary.

Because of his background, my father found it difficult to understand why native-born Americans aren't more appreciative of "this wonderful country." He asked, "Don't they realize what they have here?"

Sadly, the answer is: "No they don't. They have no comparisons."

The philanthropist-millionaire was just one generation removed from those who deeply appreciated this land of opportunity and religious freedom.

He knew they were extraordinary people who had the fortitude and vision to lay everything on the line for freedom which they did not take for granted. To them, there was nothing ordinary about being allowed to work in whatever line of endeavor they wished.

For those who had been denied this right in the "old country," this was most extraordinary.

SOME WHO APPRECIATE life the most don't have an overabundance of worldly goods. Conversely, many who supposedly enjoy the "good life" seem bored with their status. They have been affluent long enough to have forgotten what it means to do without or to pinch pennies.

Most of us seem to need reminders in all areas. Otherwise we begin taking our good fortune for granted.

Two of the happiest married people I know are also the happiest of parents.

"After five years of marriage, we had almost given up hope of having a child. And then the miracle finally happened," a lady wrote. "Amanda is here, and we are truly blessed with this beautiful baby."

Contrast this with the callous and non-appreciative attitude of too many parents who look on their offspring as nuisances who have arrived in order to cut down or curb their out-on-the-town fun time.

Some children are loved and appreciated as miracles, others are barely tolerated, if that.

THE FOLLOWING is one man's scenario for appreciating the uncommon miracle of daily life:

He awakes and knows what day it is, who he is and where he is, where he is going and what he will do when he gets there.

He doesn't have many aches and pains and realizes there are thousands of pain-wracked hospital or home-bound patients who wish they felt half as well and were able to dress themselves in order to go to work even at the spooky hour of 3:30 a.m.

He walks down the steep stairs and thinks about the wheel-chair athletes he watched on television.

He enjoys driving his smooth-running car, listening to the corny music on the radio and feeling the cool air on a still warm morning.

He remembers when houses and cars weren't air conditioned and people furiously fanned themselves and made out-of-town summer trips at night. He also recalls when the Tivoli Theater was the only air-conditioned movie house in town.

Never mind what was being shown on the big screen. The arctic air was a life saver from the humidity and heat outside.

He thinks about the statement, "You win some and you lose some" and agrees life in general is very much that way.

HE ALSO WAS AGAIN reminded so early in the morning that our Maker let each day be a new beginning with sunrise following sunset.

As he drove he realized how lucky he was to have been around for so many decades and to have done so despite shelled and mine-laden battlefields, the risk of dangerous drivers and diseases, worry and junk food addiction.

He thought perhaps there was a reason for him to be here this long and he was grateful.

He had very much enjoyed being a young man and even now

he still enjoyed the mystery and excitement of life. He realized he had learned more from mistakes, failures, hard knocks and tragedy than from the good times.

And even — perhaps especially — at this point in life, he appreciates being here on this Earth.

He sums up this appreciation as stemming from something to do, something to look forward to and someone to love.

He is learning to live in increments of moments — not just days or even hours.

He is Grabbing Life — savoring each moment — and Hanging On.

And he knows there is nothing ordinary about this.

ABOUT THE AUTHOR

Julius Parker is city editor of the Chattanooga News Free Press and author of the newspaper's widely read Sunday column, "Parker . . . and People."

A native of Chattanooga, he attended the University of Chattanooga. He served in the Army for five years and was in combat in Europe and the Philippines during World War II. Before joining the News Free Press, he held a variety of jobs including theater manager and business owner.

During a distinguished 43-year career as a journalist, he has been a feature writer, a political writer honored by the Tennessee Legislature, an editor and a columnist. He has covered eight national conventions and interviewed Presidents, statesmen and other dignitaries from all walks of life.

This book is set in 12 point New Baskerville.
Typography by The Type Shop, Inc., Chattanooga, Tennessee
Printing by Womble Printing Company, Chattanooga, Tennessee
Binding by Nicholstone Bindery, Inc., Nashville, Tennessee